高校英语选修课系列教材

PRACTICAL ENGLISH WRITING

实用英语写作

主　编　谭　键
副主编　李　丹
编　者　王晓丹　苏小青
　　　　肖　勇　孙　荧

清华大学出版社
北京

内 容 简 介

本书共五部分：第一部分申请文书，涵盖了申请留学或求职时的写作常见文体；第二部分学术写作，帮助学生提高学期论文及毕业论文的撰写能力；第三部分五段式短文，介绍经典的框架结构与基本要素，为实用文体的构思与写作奠定基础；第四部分写作备考，训练学生逐一攻克主流考试中的英语写作；第五部分写作与语法，介绍如何运用恰当的英文措辞撰写有效的英文句子，更正常见的语法错误，正确使用标点符号等。本书配套单元小测，读者可先扫描封底的"文泉云盘防盗码"解锁资源后，再扫描书中对应处的二维码获取资源，同时登录清华大学出版社"文泉考试"平台进行在线单元测验。

本书以非英语专业本科生为主要对象，也适用于有意提升英语写作水平的学习者。

版权所有，侵权必究。举报：010-62782989，beiqinquan@tup.tsinghua.edu.cn。

图书在版编目（CIP）数据

实用英语写作／谭键主编．—北京：清华大学出版社，2024.9—（高校英语选修课系列教材）．
ISBN 978-7-302-66567-0

Ⅰ.H319.36

中国国家版本馆 CIP 数据核字第 20243J0W98 号

责任编辑：徐博文
封面设计：李伯骥
责任校对：王荣静
责任印制：丛怀宇

出版发行：清华大学出版社
网　　址：https://www.tup.com.cn，https://www.wqxuetang.com
地　　址：北京清华大学学研大厦 A 座　　　邮　编：100084
社 总 机：010-83470000　　　邮　购：010-62786544
投稿与读者服务：010-62776969，c-service@tup.tsinghua.edu.cn
质量反馈：010-62772015，zhiliang@tup.tsinghua.edu.cn

印 装 者：河北鹏润印刷有限公司
经　　销：全国新华书店
开　　本：185mm×260mm　　印　张：13.75　　字　数：271 千字
版　　次：2024 年 9 月第 1 版　　印　次：2024 年 9 月第 1 次印刷
定　　价：62.00 元

产品编号：098769-01

前　言

《实用英语写作》依据《大学英语教学指南》(2020)对书面表达能力提出的具体要求设计，旨在帮助学习者掌握必要的英语写作基础知识和实用文体写作方法与技巧，从而进一步提高英语写作水平，完成从本科学习到继续深造，再到求职等阶段的必要写作知识储备，进而促进学习者的专业学习、升学就业、学术研究以及国际交流。

本书包含五个部分，即申请文书、学术写作、五段式短文、写作备考、写作与语法。五个部分共计20个单元，兼具学术性与实用性。每单元包括四个模块，分别为课前任务、引言、知识要点和写作实践，在讲授基础理论知识的同时，注重拓展学习者的思维能力、积累语言知识、提高篇章架构及写作实践能力。其中，课前任务是以任务驱动学习者的学习动机，预备学习新知识和新技能的知识框架；知识要点为每单元的知识点讲解、范文与案例分析、习作点评等；写作实践则侧重引导学习者在掌握相关知识点的同时，进行反思、总结、实践，运用英文写作思维模式，锤炼语言技能，真正提高英文写作实践的效果。教师在教学中可以融入师生、生生合作式学习模式，如头脑风暴、师生讨论、口头报告、师生互评、教师点评等，既能调动学习积极性和课堂气氛，也能促使学生相互评价、督促、激励、协作，共同提升英语写作综合能力。

本书特色

1. 本书注重培养学生广泛阅读、积极思考、发表见解、热烈讨论、相互学习等方面的学习习惯，达到在写作过程中提高学生综合能力的教学目标。

2. 知识要点环节讲解翔实，举例典型，分析具体，能切实有效地帮助学生掌握写作要领，熟悉写作规范和写作方法，语言正确得体、文体恰当、内容充实，提高表达思想的准确性与鲜明性。

3. 范文与案例符合学生学习、深造和未来工作的实际需求，容易激发学生的兴趣，利于借鉴和仿写，同时引发思考和讨论，提高学生的分析鉴赏能力和批判性、辩证性、创造性思维能力。

4. 写作实践环节设计进阶式练习，创新写作实践设计。练习形式多样：有口头练习、小组讨论、独立写作、同伴互评等，有利于教师开展各种教学活动，达到预期的教学效果。

本书编写团队制作的"实用英语写作慕课"已于2020年2月在"中国大学慕课"上线，慕课是全英文讲解，与本教材在线上线下进行教学内容的有机结合，相互补充，无缝对接。本书由西北工业大学外国语学院一线写作教学团队编写，凝聚了各位老师多年来在实用英语写作教学方面的教学经验和研究成果，也体现了我们对实用英语写作教学改革进行探索和尝试的初心。囿于编者水平有限，书中难免存在疏漏和缺点，敬请各位读者批评指正，以便再版时修订。

编　者

2024 年 5 月

Contents

Part 1 申请文书 (Application Documents Writing)

- Unit 1 简历 (Résumé) 3
- Unit 2 申请信 (Application Letter) 17
- Unit 3 推荐信 (Recommendation Letter) 27
- Unit 4 个人陈述 (Personal Statement) 31

Part 2 学术写作 (Academic Writing)

- Unit 5 学术论文的框架 (Format of Academic Research Papers) 39
- Unit 6 学术文体风格 (Academic Style) 57
- Unit 7 直接引用、改写与总结 (Quoting, Paraphrasing and Summarizing) 65
- Unit 8 模糊限制语 (Hedging Language) 73

Part 3 五段式短文 (Five-paragraph Essay Writing)

- Unit 9 五段式短文简介 (An Introduction to Five-paragraph Essay) 79
- Unit 10 谋篇布局 (Planning an Essay) 85
- Unit 11 完成初稿 (Drafting) 93
- Unit 12 修改 (Revising) 109

Part 4 写作备考 (Writing for Tests)

- Unit 13 大学英语四、六级写作 (Writing for CET-4 and CET-6) 119
- Unit 14 雅思写作 (Writing for IELTS) 127

Unit 15 托福写作（Writing for TOEFL） 139

Unit 16 考研英语写作（Writing for National Postgraduate Entrance Examination） 153

Part 5 写作与语法（Writing and Grammar）

Unit 17 词汇（Diction） 167
Unit 18 句子（Sentence） 177
Unit 19 语法（Grammar） 189
Unit 20 标点（Punctuation） 203

第一部分　申请文书
Part 1　Application Documents Writing

内容提要
Preview

第一部分着重介绍英文写作中具有特殊或实用目的的写作形式，共四单元。第 1 单元是个人简历，第 2 单元是求职信 / 求学申请信，第 3 单元是为求职 / 求学人员提供的推荐信，第 4 单元是申请求学 / 求职时需要递交的个人陈述。以上四类是公文写作中展示个人学识、能力及资历的重要形式，该部分突出写作的实际应用性，注重写作格式、特点及语言表达策略。每部分配有可读性与可操作性的范例，加以辅助说明。通过该部分的讲练结合，学习者能够了解申请文书的主要类型及其特征，并掌握相应的写作规范。

第 1 单元　简历
Unit 1　Résumé

学习目标 Learning Objectives

1. 了解简历的概念与功能；
2. 熟悉简历的主要构成部分与写作要点。

课前任务 Pretask

请找出并仔细阅读几份英文简历，观察其主要构成与写作特点，并总结简历与其他申请文书的写作区别。

引言 Introduction

简历（résumé）又称履历或个人简历，顾名思义，是对个人经历的简要记录。在英语中，简历主要有两种表达方式：一种是较为常见的 résumé，源于法语，意为 summary（总结）；另一种是多为学术界常用的 curriculum vitae，源于拉丁语，简写为 CV 或 C.V.，一般用于申请教师、研究员等学术职位。简历是介绍个人基本情况、学业资历、工作经验等信息的文字材料，是求职者自我展示的一种形式，也是用人单位判断求职者是否为本单位需要人才的依据。本单元主要介绍简历的主要功能、特点、基本结构和写作要点。

知识要点 Key Knowledge

1.1　简历的功能（Functions of Résumé）

简历可以广泛应用于各类正式交际场合中，是建立个人整体形象、展示个人优点强项的工具。就求职而言，一封写作规范、重点突出的简历可以帮助求职者快速吸引用人单位的注意，使用人单位了解求职者的成长轨迹、教育背景、工作经历、主要业绩、优势特长等。

注意： 简历并不一定能够确保求职者获得某个职位或项目，但可以作为"敲门砖"帮助求职者获得宝贵的面试机会，以便进一步"推销"自己。换句话说，简历是招聘人员或雇主对求职者的第一印象。因此，撰写简历是申请工作或求职应聘过程中至关重要的第一步。

1.2 简历的特点（Features of Résumé）

作为一种特殊的公文写作文体，无论从结构上或是语言上，简历均和其他文体有较大区别，具体表现在三个方面：

1.2.1 客观性（Objectiveness）

简历是求职者个人身份与背景经历的概括总结，是个人整体形象的缩影，因此应客观、全面、真实、准确地反映个人信息，如教育背景、工作经历、经验资历、荣誉获奖等，在帮助自己获取适合的工作职位的同时，不能误导甚至欺骗用人单位。

1.2.2 凝练性（Conciseness）

投递简历的目的是为了让用人单位在短时间内获取求职者的主要和重要信息，并决定该求职者能否进入下一轮面试。一份繁杂冗长的简历无法快速吸引人的眼球，更不能传递最关键的信息。简历应简短、凝练，以一页篇幅为宜，结构清晰，重点突出，言简意赅。简历中不用把个人的全部情况一一罗列，而应高度概括，更多聚焦与应聘岗位相关或对用人单位有价值的信息，既能给人正面积极的第一印象，也便于招聘人员获取重点信息。

1.2.3 独特性（Uniqueness）

简历虽有一定的写作规范，但如果求职者希望自己脱颖而出，可以考虑简历的个体性和独特性，包括个人独特或优越的学习和工作经历，与求职岗位高度匹配的特质资历等。同时，也应针对不同岗位设计简历内容，使简历所呈现出的个人特点与资历具有针对性，符合岗位要求，并富有创意与新意，获取用人单位的好感和认可。

1.3 简历的类型（Styles of Résumé）

根据呈现形式，简历可分为表格型和文字型。表格型简历简洁清晰，一目了然，但形式略显单一；文字型简历则更常见。根据其功能和目的，文字性简历又可分为三类：时间顺序型、功能型、混合型。

1.3.1 时间顺序型（Chronological）

顾名思义，时间顺序型简历中的教育背景、工作经历、业绩成就等各个部分均采用由近及远的时间顺序进行罗列,既明确体现求职者当前的状况,又清晰呈现出其成长与发展的时间轴,一般较为适合工作经历丰富且业绩显著的求职者。

范例[1]:

Employment

Medical Transcriptionist

Foothill Family Counseling Center-21297 Foothill Blvd., Suite 100, Hayward, CA

September 2020—Present

Effectively download, transcribe, and revise dictation using Express Scribe or eScription software; Provide secure download and maintaining of sensitive materials via Google Drive and Windows 8.1 with encryption; Acute attention to detail in the transcription and revision processes to maintain a low error risk level.

Sergeant Scout Sniper Team Leader

United States Marine Corps-2nd Battalion, 1st Marines, Camp Pendleton, CA

May 2017—September 2020

Employed a scout sniper team in support of Battalion and MEU operations; Effectively employed the M40-A5, M110 SASS, and M107 SASR to detect, select, and reduce key targets and targets of opportunity in support of combat operations; Effectively employed the MAGTF Secondary Imaging Dissemination System. Applied effective communication with HF, VHF, UHF, and SATCOM systems.

Executive Board Member of Fraternity

Illinois State University-100 North University Street, Normal, IL

August 2015—May 2017

Served on Chi Omega Fraternity Executive Board, organized and directed members in rush activities. Established various motivational activities. Prepared payment plans for sorority members and oversaw savings and checking accounts. Trained employees for duties in Canteen Lunch Restaurant.

---

1 来自《谷歌学术》官方网站。

1.3.2 功能型（Functional）

功能型简历一般围绕求职岗位的特征和用人单位的需求，重点呈现个人资质、能力、成就等，而非采用传统简历中的固定模块和时间顺序排列。这种简历可吸引招聘人员快速获取求职者与岗位需求匹配的相关信息，一般更适合工作经历较为单一或工作更换相对频繁的求职者。

范例[1]：

Leadership

Selected Speaker, PanEl Symposium, Colby-Sawyer College

April 2011

- Selected to participate in conference comparing and contrasting cultures in Asia.

President & Founder, Cross Cultural Club September

April 2010—Present

- Founded club to provide forum for sharing cultures and promoting inter-cultural understanding;
- Conducted meetings and developed projects to foster participation in activities;
- Initiated first Colby-Sawyer International Night featuring various cuisine and entertainment.

Guest Speaker, Concord Elementary School, Concord, NH

October 2011

- Requested to introduce students to Korean life styles, culture, and basic socio-economic conditions.

Volunteer, New London Conservation Commission

October 2011

1.3.3 混合型（Combined）

混合型简历结合了时间顺序型和功能型的优点，在各模块延续时间顺序的同时，突出表现求职者能够胜任该岗位的过人资质和显著优势，以达到简洁有序而又重点突出的目的。

---

[1] 来自《谷歌学术》官方网站。

1.4 简历的结构（Structure of Résumé）

简历的基本结构和内容没有统一固定的模式，但为了给人快速留下良好的第一印象，在遵循一定框架模式的同时，也应保持写作规范和语言特色。一般而言，简历的基本结构通常包括六个主要部分：个人信息、求职目标、教育背景、工作经历、专长和业绩、推荐人。

1.4.1 个人信息（Personal Information）

范例：

> Elaine Ford
>
> 124th Street
>
> Overland Park, Kansas 06020
>
> 709-4207-2155
>
> eford@gmail.com

由上例可见，简历第一部分的个人信息一般包括姓名（name）、地址（address）、联系电话（phone number）、电子邮箱地址（email address）等。该部分主要提供求职者的基本信息和联系方式，个人信息应全面、直观、清晰、简洁。

注意：（1）尽可能提供详细的个人信息；

（2）使用永久地址，而非临时地址；

（3）联系电话除手机号码外，还可提供固定电话号码，并附区号；

（4）提供正式的电子邮箱地址（如学校邮箱）；

（5）涉及个人隐私的信息则不必一一列出。

1.4.2 求职目标（Objective of Application）

简历中应明确、醒目、具体地写出求职目标，这既是对个人清晰合理地定位，又能使招聘人员准确了解求职者的意向。求职者不必顾虑太过明确的求职目标会限制自己被调剂到其他行业或部门的可能性，事实上，太过宽泛的求职目标反而使招聘人员难以确定求职者的优势和个人倾向，认为求职者对自身缺乏明晰的定位。因此，简历应呈现出针对某个岗位"量身定制"般的资历和经验，个人定位应准确成熟，目标明确笃定，而非笼统模糊、广而泛之地投递简历。

例如：

Objective: To work as an entry-level computer programmer in a financial institution

一个明确的求职目标包括求职者的岗位意向（如程序员、会计、秘书等）、级别意向（如实习生、助理、中层管理人员等），以及领域或行业意向（如教育或金融机构、航空航天行业等）。简历中的求职目标可以表述为申请职业（Profession Applied for）或目标职位（Position Wanted/Desired），但均应尽量具体，以达到同等效果。

例如：

Position Wanted: A position in the Finance Department which requires skills in finance software application and work experience

关于岗位名称的常见表达有：

- 助理教授 / 副教授 / 教授（assistant professor/associate professor/professor）
- 实习医生 / 主治医师 / 主任医师（intern/attending doctor/chief physician）
- 软件 / 硬件工程师（software/hardware engineer）
- 市场开发 / 营销经理（market development manager/marketing manager）
- 总会计师 / 财务总监（chief accountant/financial controller）
- 行政助理 / 业务主管 / 业务经理（administrative assistant/business controller/business manager）

1.4.3 教育背景（Educational Background）

教育背景指求职者接受教育的经历和相关情况，一般包括院校名称和在校学习的起止时间（若求职者尚未毕业，可注明即将毕业的时间）、学位名称（如理学学士、工商管理硕士等）、专业（主修、辅修）等。列举顺序一般从最高学历开始，由近及远，直至大学本科（高中及以下学习经历一般无须纳入）。

对于刚毕业且尚不具有从业经验的应届毕业生或工作经历较为短暂的求职者而言，应该首先在简历中醒目地列出其教育背景（对于申请入职教育机构的求职者来说尤为重要），并尽量包含与申请工作相关或符合岗位要求的选修课程，以及从中获取的知识与技能。根据实际情况或岗位需要，还可酌情列出求职者的GPA（平均绩点）及排名情况，或外语水平、国外学习交流经历等。

例如：

Bachelor of Arts, University of North Carolina, Chapel Hill, NC,

December 2016

Major: Psychology

Minor: Political Science

Overall GPA: 3.9 (Top 5%)

注意：（1）简历应扬长避短。例如，若求职者的 GPA 较高，可列出具体分数，并附上排名或量化的评价标准，如"专业前 5%"，以增强说服力；反之则可避之不提。

（2）说明排名情况时，一般可同时注明个人排名及全年级人数，进一步增强说服力，如"排名：6/150"。

（3）若求职者是硕士或博士研究生，应尽量写出当前的研究方向，甚至可包括学位论文（thesis/dissertation）题目；若有论文、课题等相关学术成果，尤其正好与应聘岗位相关的，也应一并列出。

关于教育背景的常见表达有：

- 本科生 / 研究生（undergraduate student/graduate student）
- 必修课 / 选修课 / 专业课（compulsory course/elective course/specialized course）
- 文学学士 / 理学学士 (Bachelor of Arts, B.A.)/ (Bachelor of Science, B.S.)
- 文学硕士 / 工学硕士 / 理学硕士 (Master of Arts，M.A.)/ (Master of Engineering，M.E.)/ (Master of Science，M.S.)
- 工学博士 / 哲学博士 / 理学博士 (Doctor of Engineering，E.D.)/ (Doctor of Philosophy，Ph.D.) / (Doctor of Science，S.D.)
- 博士后 (Postdoctorate，Postdoc)

1.4.4 工作经历（Work Experience）

工作经历是简历中的重要部分，主要概述求职者获得技能和能力的工作经历，一般包括起止时间、工作单位与部门名称、所在地、职务职位、工作职责、工作业绩等。工作经历的顺序与教育背景类似，一般按倒序由近及远排列。

工作经历不仅指正式工作经历，对于尚未毕业的大学生而言，也可涉及其他类型的实习或实践经验，如学校社团的工作经历，或在某个大型活动中担任志愿者，以及其他类似的课外活动，相应的"工作单位"名称可以是社团、组织机构或某组委会的名称。为强调求职者通过工作经历所获取的具体技能或成就，在描述工作职责时最好使用表示能力的行为动词（action verb），如"管理（manage）""负责（charge）""开发（develop）"等。最为重要的是，应尽可能多地列举与应聘岗位相关的工作经历，以进一步增强求职者能够胜任所申请职位的说服力。

关于实践经历的行为动词有：

- 学生会（student union）
- 实习 / 业余工作 / 志愿者活动（internship/part-time job/volunteer work）
- 计划 / 提议 / 培训 / 开发（planned/proposed/trained/developed）
- 运作 / 组织 / 管理 / 协助（operated/organized/managed/assisted）
- 产出 / 创造 / 完成 / 表现 / 展示（produced/created/completed/performed/presented）
- 增加 / 加大 / 提升 / 扩展（increased/enlarged/enhanced/expanded）

1.4.5 专长和业绩（Specialization and Achievements）

该部分是为了展示个人最突出的优势与强项，应尽量选取和申请职位相关的业绩和获奖，以证明个人的突出能力。求职者应该根据岗位需求有针对性地写特长，而不是泛泛提及热爱阅读（reading）、旅行（traveling）、听音乐（listening to music）等陈词滥调。同时，描述既要实事求是，也要明确获奖或业绩的实质，强调奖励的级别、受资助情况，也可用数字说明该奖项或业绩的难度与含金量，并包括活动或比赛的名称、获奖级别以及日期等，同样采用倒叙排列。

范例：

- 荣获2019年"外研社·国才杯"全国英语写作比赛省级决赛一等奖（First-Prize Winner at Provincial Final of the 2019 "FLTRP·ETIC Cup" English Writing Contest）
- 获2020年度全国教育系统先进工作者称号（Advanced Worker of the 2020 National Higher Education）

1.4.6 推荐人（References）

简历的最后有时会提供推荐人信息，包括推荐人的姓名、单位、职务、职称、学位、联系方式等。推荐人可以是对求职者背景与资历较为了解的领导、同事等，或相应专业或行业的专家、教授和资深人士，能对求职者给出准确合理的评价。值得一提的是，在简历中列出推荐人必须征得其同意，注明方便与推荐人联系的合适时间。一个更为简单的策略是，在简历底部注明"专家推荐人，索函即寄（References upon request）"。

虽然简历的以上六个部分同等重要，但求职者可根据所申请的岗位需求与特征重点强调其中某一个部分。若申请学习项目或学术型机构岗位，简历可强调教育背景与学业表现；

若申请重视从业经验的专业技术或管理岗位，则应突出工作经验和成果业绩，也可以根据不同的工作类型来强调不同的经历、经验或业绩奖励。

1.5 如何写出成功的简历（How to Write a Successful Résumé）

在面临激烈的竞争时，一份优秀的简历对于成功申请学业或工作机会至关重要。若要增加求职者脱颖而出的概率，一份成功的简历应该具备以下特点：

（1）**篇幅简短**。为使招聘人员能够在短时间内获得关键有效的信息，了解申请人的资历优势，简历的篇幅不应过长，以一页篇幅为宜，最多不超过两页。

（2）**重点突出**。简历的目的是为了树立个人的良好形象，突出呈现申请人能够胜任该岗位的优势，因此应针对求职目标，筛选关键信息。

（3）**语言凝练**。简历中的语言表达应简明扼要、准确具体，句子和段落均不宜过长，多使用平行结构（parallel structure）来表述相关或并列内容，可省略第一人称代词、情态动词、冠词、介词短语等；尽量使用行为动词/短语描述工作或活动，突出申请人的专业能力。

（4）**版式清晰**。简洁大方的简历版式能够吸引阅读兴趣，提升快速阅读，因此简历的版面设计应美观端庄，层次清晰，结构分明，格式规范；可使用不同的字体来强调不同版块的主题和内容，并有适当留白，使招聘人员能够一目了然地获取关键信息，并体现出申请人的审美品位与文化素养，给人留下良好的第一印象。

（5）**关注细节**。细节决定成败。简历中一个小小的语言错误就能反映出申请人的粗心大意和专业不足。因此，简历中的表述应简洁明了，用词准确，精益求精，不能过度夸大，更不能充斥着语病和错别字。

1.6 简历范例（Sample Résumés）

1.6.1 时间顺序型（Chronological）

范例[1]：

Artist Sample Resume

220 Broome Street, New York, NY 10013

(212) 684-2473

john.doe@gmail.com

Artist with 3 years of related work experience, as well as portfolio of varied

---

[1] 来自《谷歌学术》官方网站。

accomplishments including referenced articles, exhibitions, and academic achievements. Possess a strong sense of artistry and forward-thinking, that is consistently displayed across all art pieces. Capable of communicating with clients regarding specifications for customized art pieces.

▶▶ Education

Master of Fine Arts in Industrial Art　　　　　　　　　　　　　San Francisco, CA
Academy of Art University，May 2014

- Top prize in university's art competition, 2013

Bachelor of Fine Arts in Studio Art and Art History　　　　　　　Philadelphia, PA
University of the Arts，May 2012

- Graduated Cum Laude
- Honor Roll and Distinction

▶▶ Professional Experience

Self-employed New York, NY

Artist (Freelance), June 2013—Present

- Design, develop, and deliver art pieces to clients according to specifications
- Create abstract sculptures to be displayed in local establishments
- Produce stylized and realistic photos for 3 online websites
- Collaborate with local museum to develop and fit art installations across outside area

▶▶ Mexic-arte Museum Austin, TX

Collections Cataloguer, August 2012—May 2013

- Catalogued a total of 1,200 items according to different categories, completing project 30 days ahead of schedule
- Analyzed database record and ensured integrity of bibliographic contents
- Re-wrote new descriptions for 30% of items that were outdated or had insufficient information

▶▶ Bibliography

- Linda Krasinski, "A New Point of View", *The Guardian*, February 2013
- William J. Bore, "Crossing the Lines", Sculpture 19, No. 1, October 2011

▶▶ Exhibitions

- Solo Exhibition: Thesis Exhibition, John Kempt Gallery
- Two-Person Exhibition: Moore Contemporary, New York, NY (with industrial artist Lisa Meyer)

▶▶ Additional Skills

- Photography and Sculpture
- Adobe Photoshop

1.6.2 混合型（Combined）

范例[1]：

Susie Student

Campus Address: Room 999, Lawson Hall; Phone: X 9999

Home Address: 321 Main Street, Anywhere US 12345

(603) 526-3000

sstudent@my.colby-sawyer.edu

▶▶ Objective

To provide leadership in a Resident Assistant position

▶▶ Education

Bachelor of Fine Arts: Studio Art, Psychology Minor	Anticipated May 2014
Colby-Sawyer College	New London, NH
Cumulative GPA: 3.5, Dean's List	

▶▶ Experience

Counselor/Art Instructor	June—August 2009—2011
Camp Matapони Naples, ME	

- Provided leadership, discipline and counseling services to residents of a recreational summer camp
- Ensured safety, well being of campers and created an atmosphere of respect and acceptance

---

1 来自《谷歌学术》官方网站。

- Directly supervised up to 40 campers aged 6-15
- Planned and led children through art projects
- Designed and painted props, sets and programs for small theater productions

Delivery Driver December 2009—Present

Pizza Joint

- Demonstrated strong customer service skills   Portland, Maine
- Answered telephone inquiries, completed orders and transactions using a computer
- Handled multiple tasks in a very busy atmosphere
- Received two merit increases for exceptional performance

Prep Cook/Line Cook (Seasonal)   December 2009—January 2010

Stowe Mountain Resort   Stowe, VT

Screen Printer/Quality Inspector/Office Assistant   August 2008—September 2009

Tubbs Snowshoe Company   Stowe, VT

▶▶ Activities September 2010—Present

Class Officer, Class of 2014

- Co-President 2011—2012; Secretary 2010—2011

Student Government Association September 2008—May 2009

- Senator 2009
- Treasurer and Allocations Committee Chair 2008—2009

Varsity Track and Field May 2011

History, Society and Culture Club September 2010—Present

- Treasurer 2010—2011

Safe Zones September 2011—Present

- Treasurer 2011—2012

Student Representative, Alumni Council Spring 2012

Honors Advisory Committee Student Member September 2011—Present

Social Sciences Professor Search Committee Member January 2011—April 2011

Orientation Leader August 2011—September 2011

▶▶ Leadership

Selected Speaker, PanEl Symposium, Colby-Sawyer College   April 2011

- Selected to participate in conference comparing and contrasting cultures in Asia

President & Founder, Cross Cultural Club September　　　　　　2010—Present
- Founded club to provide forum for sharing cultures and promoting inter-cultural understanding
- Conducted meetings and developed projects to foster participation in activities
- Initiated first Colby-Sawyer International Night featuring various cuisine and entertainment

Guest Speaker, Concord Elementary School, Concord, NH　　　　October 2011
- Requested to introduce students to Korean life styles, culture, and basic socio-economic conditions

Volunteer, New London Conservation Commission　　　　　　　October 2011

▶▶ **Volunteer Experience**

Maine General Hospital Augusta, ME　　　　　　January 2009—August 2009
- Assisted with upkeep of a physical therapy facility
- Prepared work areas for clients and therapist

Hanna House Hanover, NH　　　　　　　October 2009—December 2009
- Assisted staff at a residential facility for adolescent mothers and their children
- Helped teen mothers with time management and organization of daily chores

▶▶ **References**

References are available on request

【解析】以上两封求职简历分别采用时间顺序型和混合型，内容完整，包括个人基本信息、教育背景、工作经历、技能优势、志愿者经历、推荐信息等，条目清晰，细节详尽，语言精练，着重教育背景和工作经历中与申请职位相符的相关情况，重点突出，有说服力。

写作实践 Writing Tasks

▶▶ **Writing Practice 1**

Based on your major and future plan, combined with your qualifications and advantages, write a résumé for a job position you intend to apply for. Pay special attention to the educational background and internship experience that match the applied position.

▶▶ **Writing Practice 2**

Write a résumé for applying for the job position as a software engineer in an eminent research institute based on the introduction of Zhou Jie below. You may add some detailed information about the applicant where necessary.

周杰，2021年博士毕业于华东师范大学计算机科学与技术学院，2016年硕士毕业于浙江大学计算机专业。曾获"上海市大学生年度人物"荣誉、华东师范大学校长奖学金。在世界顶级期刊上发表论文20余篇，谷歌学术引用超过130次。曾7次参与国内外知名大数据挖掘比赛，4次获得冠军，在联合国教科文组织和百度联合举办的"一带一路"国际大数据比赛中获得特等奖。研究成果应用于社会多个领域，多次在国际顶级会议作口头报告。[1]

---

1 来自《中国青年报》《人民资讯》官方网站。

第 2 单元　申请信
Unit 2　Application Letter

学习目标 Learning Objectives

1. 掌握英文正式信函的格式；
2. 了解申请信的特点与功能；
3. 掌握申请信的主要构成部分与写作要点。

课前任务 Pretask

熟悉正式英文信函的格式特点，学习申请信与私人信函的区别以及求职申请信与求学申请信的区别。

引言 Introduction

申请信（application letter）是在申请入学资格、奖学金或工作岗位时随简历一同递交学校或用人单位的信函，有时也被称为附函（cover letter），相当于一篇全面、简洁且遵循一定写作格式的自我介绍。申请信通常分为两类：求学申请信（application letter for admission）和求职申请信（application letter for employment），主要内容包括写信目的、个人资历与优势、未来规划或贡献等。本单元将主要介绍英文申请信的结构、特点、功能和写作要点。

知识要点 Key Knowledge

2.1　申请信的结构（Structure of a Application Letter）

在信息化的今天，人们在各类社交媒体的辅助下可以轻松地与他人联系，但有时仍然需要通过电子邮件或纸质信函进行沟通，因为邮件或信函更为正式，也更易于追踪。申请信是一封正式信函，有别于私人信件。在了解申请信的正式写法之前，应首先掌握英文正式信函的格式和惯例。

正式信函通常由六个基本部分组成：信头、地址、称呼语、正文、结束语和签名，有时也会包括附件和附言，可被视为结束语的一部分。

范例[1]：

Marler Information Network
3131 Longwood Ave., P.O. Box 461
Kelso, Washington 97987
(800) 555-4647
101 1994
　　　　　　　　　　　　　　　　——信头

Ms. Tabatha Mead
Account Representative
Sky Chief Productions
31 Dogwood Ct.
Corvallis, OR 97876
　　　　　　　　　　　　　　　　——信内地址

Dear Ms. Mead:　　　　——称呼语

It has been several weeks since our last correspondence, and we have made great strides in developing our new computerized accounts network.

…

Thank you for your kind attention to this matter. We look forward to working with you.
　　　　　　　　　　　　　　　　——正文

Sincerely yours,　　　　——结束敬语

Signature
James Marler
President/CEO　　　　——落款/签名

Encl. The contract of the data network.　——附件

---

[1] 来自《谷歌学术》官方网站。

2.1.1 信头（Heading）

信头通常出现在信函的第一页顶端或右上角，包括写信人的单位名称、完整地址和写信日期。在公函中，信纸上通常会印有写信人所在单位或机构的名称、地址、电话号码、传真号码、网站、微信公众号以及该单位的标志（logo），这种信函的信头部分只需要写出日期即可。如果是私人正式信函，须将本人地址按照一定的规范顺序写在信纸的右上角，并在顶端部分留出一定的空白区域。英文地名的顺序是从小到大排列，即门牌号—街道—地区—城市—省或州—国家。信头和信内地址的格式包括齐头式（block format）和缩进式（indented format）两种。

范例：

齐头式

School of Foreign Studies
Northwestern Polytechnical University
127 West Youyi Road, Beilin District,
Xi'an, Shaanxi 710065
P. R. China

缩进式

School of Foreign Studies
　　Northwestern Polytechnical University
　　　　127 West Youyi Road, Beilin District,
　　　　　　Xi'an, Shaanxi 710065
　　　　　　　　P. R. China

信函日期应在写信人地址下方另起一行的位置。英国写法常为日/月/年，如 12 May, 2022；美国写法常为月/日/年，如 May 12, 2022。同时还应注意，正式信函中日期的月份名称须完整，不可使用缩写，如 11 月 13 日应写为"13 November/November 13,"而非"13 Nov./Nov. 13"。

2.1.2 信内地址（Inside Address）

信内地址一般包括收信人的姓名和完整地址，通常在第一页信纸的左上方，信头和日期的下一行。信内地址一般用于正式信函，而非私人信件。此外，为表示尊重，收件人的姓名前一般应加上敬语或头衔,如在男士的姓名前加"Mr.",在女士的姓名前加"Ms.",或根据收件人的职务或头衔加"Prof.""Dr."等。如不确定收件人身份,则可直接写对方职务名称,如"经理(Manager)""编辑(Editor)"等。

2.1.3 称呼语(Salutation)

称呼语是对收信人的敬称,通常与左边空白处齐平,在信内地址下方两行顶格的位置。无论是正式信函还是私人信件,都应包含称呼语。称呼语一般包括收件人的头衔加姓氏,如"Dear Ms. Smith"或"Dear Prof. Lee"等。在初次信函往来时,如果不知道收件人的姓名,可使用"Dear Sir/Madam",或使用职务名称,如上文提及的"Manager、Editor"等,也可以直接使用"To whom it may concern"等惯用称呼。此外,称呼语后的标点符号在私人信件中多用逗号,而在正式或商务信函中多用冒号。

2.1.4 正文(Body)

正文是信函的主体部分,一般在低于称呼语一两行处,通常有三种格式:齐头式(block format)、缩进式(indented format)、混合式(mixed format)。在齐头式中,每个段落的第一行都从左边对齐,段落内部使用单倍行间距,段落之间需要空一行。在缩进式中,每个段落的第一行缩进5个字符。写信人可以选择个人偏好的风格,但整封信函应保持一致。混合式是前两种格式的结合体,一般标题居中,日期、敬语及签名右对齐,正文每段的第一行左对齐或统一缩进。这种格式既方便又美观,也因此更为常见。

2.1.5 结束敬语(Complimentary Close)

结束敬语是写信人在信尾处对收件人的敬语,一般单独成段,置于正文后一到两行,可以左对齐,也可以居中。通常开头第一个单词的首字母须大写,结尾处加逗号。此外,结束敬语应与收件人的称呼一致。例如,给正式机构写信时,可以用"Yours sincerely""Faithfully yours"等;给年长者或资历高于本人者写信时,可以用"Yours respectfully";给家人朋友写信时,则可用"Yours cordially""With love""Take care"等。

2.1.6 签名(Signature)

一般情况下,在纸质的商务信函中应有写信人的亲笔签名,以示正式或承诺。手写签名一般在结束敬语和打印的姓名落款之间,通常在结尾下方的一两行处。注意:如落款姓名是中文名,手写签名应该是中文姓名的拼音,而不是英文名。

2.1.7 附件(Enclosure)和附言(Postscript)

若写信人想随信附上其他文件,如简历、成绩单或证书等,可以在签名下方、信纸的左下角用"Enclosure/Encl."注明附件，以提醒收件人查阅。若写信人想补充说明其他信息，则可用附言，一般置于信纸左下角、签名下方一两行处，由缩写字母 P.S. 或 PS 开头，接着写出需要补充的内容。

2.2 求职申请信（Application Letter for Employment）

在正式信函中，使用频率最高的一般为申请信，通常分为求职申请信与求学申请信两类。这两类申请信一版都包括三个部分：第一个部分写明申请信的目的，如申请某个职位或申请入学、奖学金等，可提及获取信息的渠道以及个人对用人单位或学校的了解；第二个部分旨在向申请单位或学校陈述并强调个人的资历与优势，证明自己能够胜任的理由，以及未来能做的贡献；第三个部分主要表达申请人的希望，如请对方考虑自己的申请或给予面试的机会等。

2.2.1 求职信的特点（Features）

（1）**自荐性**。求职申请信最基本的特点是自我推荐性，应实事求是地陈述个人情况，对标岗位要求，充分展示自己的综合素养和特长。此外，求职信还可兼具创新性和个性化，给招聘人员留下深刻和良好的印象。

（2）**得体性**。作为交流方式的一种，信函写作应注意与对方的书面交流。在内容上，应做到主题明确，结构清晰，重点突出，论证有力，使对方可以快速获取关键信息；在语言上，对自己的评价应得体适当，既不能夸大其词，也不必妄自菲薄，整体体现个人修养与沟通能力。

（3）**格式性**。求职申请信是一种正式信函，应遵循正式信函的书写格式，必须包含称呼语、正文、结束敬语、联系方式、附件或附言等，以充分体现信函的规范性和严谨性。

（4）**简要性**。和简历类似，求职申请信也应简洁明了，内容重点突出，结构层次分明，语言准确凝练，阅读流畅舒适。

2.2.2 求职申请信的结构（Structure）

求职申请信通常由三部分组成：导言、正文和结束语。

（1）**导言**。首先，申请人在申请信开头部分应直接明确地说明写信的目的，包括应聘该单位或申请该岗位的原因等。此外，为引起招聘人员的注意力或获得好感，申请人也可以简要说明自己对该单位的了解，如该单位正在实施的新项目或出台的新政策，也可以引用一些关于该公司的积极评价等。这一部分的内容应该开门见山，语言简洁。

范例：

> XXX
>
> UNESCO
>
> China
>
> May 16, 2022
>
>   As a student from the School of Software Engineering, Northwestern Polytechnical University, I'm writing to seek for a position in the internship programme posted on *China Daily* which especially targets at graduate and postgraduate students. I have always heard about UNESCO, and the precious experience as an intern in such an exceptional organization is bound to make the best of myself.

  这个范例包含了申请人的就读学校、申请人获取该单位招聘资讯的渠道、申请人对该单位的了解及其目标岗位。

  （2）正文。正文是申请信的核心部分，旨在说明并强调申请人的个人资历、技能专长、未来展望等，尤其强调申请人的背景与岗位要求的契合度。

  个人资历条件介绍可包括教育背景、工作或实习经历，并做到就重避轻、有的放矢。例如，对于即将毕业的应届生，可以避开工作经历等薄弱方面，重点列出学历、课程、成绩等学习经历，在校期间曾经参加过的与岗位要求相关的学科竞赛、实习实践以及相关的荣誉获奖、资格证书、成果业绩等，以证明自己所具有的知识背景和专业能力。如果是有一定工作经验的求职者，应简要阐述与该岗位相关的工作经历，尤其是与应聘岗位相吻合的技能和成就。此外，该部分也可简要提及应聘单位的特点，显示申请人对应聘单位的了解以及对申请岗位的重视。如有必要，申请人也可提供一份推荐信。

  该部分应注意统一性与说服力，所涉及的学位、专业领域、技能、优势等信息都应紧紧围绕申请岗位。例如，若申请教学职位，可以列出在培训机构担任教师等类似的实习或兼职工作经历，而餐馆服务员或发放广告传单的工作经验则不必提及。若该岗位需要特殊能力或素质，也可有针对性地列出个人所具有的相关资历。例如，在申请人力资源部相关岗位时，可以重点强调申请人在协调沟通等方面的能力；在申请办公室秘书岗位时，可以提到计算机或办公软件的熟练操作程度；在申请外资企业的岗位时，则应该突出英语水平。

范例：

> In a bid to prove that I am competent for the vocation, I will make a brief introduction of myself as follows. First and foremost, I have studied English since my childhood, and my capacity has been tested by countless high standards of examinations. Given that all the results went well, it is my firm belief that I am reliable to interact with others in English. In addition, I took the intercultural communication course last term so as to develop an interest in the comparative study of nonverbal behaviors, values, identity in diversity cultures. In the issue, I will treasure the opportunity to experience the distinctions on my own.
>
> Furthermore, there are other aspects about me that give rise to my fitness for the internship chance. As I major in electrical and information engineering, I have been enabled to get familiar with a considerable number of software. As a result, my rich experience in coping with computers certainly becomes my advantages over other applicants. On top of that, dating back to the days in my senior high school, my role model was Marie Colvin, a female war journalist. I was deeply touched by her devotion to speaking for the weak as well as her love for the poor; subsequently, I even wrote a short novel to memorize her. For this reason, instead of shrinking from my responsibilities, I sincerely hope this internship will provide me with the chance to fulfill my obligation to serve the public, assist people in need, and contribute my own share to make a better world.
>
> Last but not least, practice if generally regarded as being of great importance. Although my only related experience is supporting the education of several children in rural areas, l will make every endeavor to polish myself up in the internship. Not to mention this experience will definitely lead to the cultivation of my better interpretation of UNESCO.

在这份求职信范例中，申请人对教育背景、工作经历以及在此过程中获得的技能与经验分别加以阐释，有力证明了申请人具备胜任该项工作的综合素质与能力。

（3）**结束语**。一般放在最后一段，申请人在求职信的结束段重申自己具备胜任该岗位的资历，并主动提出面试相关事宜，有时可以一并提及能够联系到本人的最佳时间。此外，也可对收信人表达谢意，体现出申请人的礼貌与素养。

例如：

I will be available in the next six months, sincerely hoping I could meet you at the interview.

Thank you for your time and consideration.

Yours sincerely,

XXX

2.3 求学申请信（Application Letter for Admission）

求学申请信和求职申请信就格式和框架均有较大的相似度。当计划申请在海外高校或其他教育机构深造或交流的项目时，学校或机构的招生部门一般会要求申请人提交一套材料，包括申请信、个人陈述、英语水平测试成绩、学业成绩单及推荐信等。

求学申请信要简明扼要地总结申请人的教育背景和专业经验，强调学业、实践等方面的获奖或荣誉，以证明自己是一位优秀的候选人。申请信中应包含写信的目的或申请的项目、申请人的突出优势与资质、申请人的未来期望与态度决心三个要点，并分别阐释说明。

范例：

> I am a Master degree student of the Software Engineering Department, Northwestern Polytechnical University, one of the leading higher learning institutions in the mainland China. I now wish to scale higher intellectual heights by pursuing Ph.D. study in your quality program of School of Computer Science and am writing to ask for a package documents. Your assistance will be greatly appreciated.
>
> I gained acceptance into Northwestern Polytechnical University in 2015. Then in the four years since, I have been receiving systematical and comprehensive training in computer science. In the fall of 2019, I began my research in Northwestern Polytechnical University. My research filed is computer security and I am at present writing my degree paper on how to protect information in the computer. I have published a book with my supervisor.

在这份申请信范例中，申请人首先表明了写信的目的，并介绍了姓名、国籍、教育背景等个人信息。在正文部分，申请人介绍其未来学习计划，包括专业、研究领域、攻读学位以及奖学金申请等。申请人需要简明扼要地阐述其优势，尤其在相关研究领域所取得的成果、奖项或技能，以证明未来有能力胜任该项目的研究工作。

2.4 如何写出成功的申请信（How to Write a Successful Application Letter）

为了使自己能够在成百上千封申请信中得以凸显，吸引招聘或招生人员的注意，并打动他们，一封成功的求职信应该具备以下特点：

2.4.1 目的明确（Distinct Objective）

清楚说明申请的工作岗位或学习项目，表明申请人具体明晰的目标。

2.4.2 内容全面（Comphrehensive Content）

全面介绍和阐释个人的资历、能力、技能等，包括知识背景、学习和工作经历、技能和能力、奖项和荣誉等。

2.4.3 风格得体（Appropriate Style）

简短而具体，礼貌而热情，简单而个性。具体而言，申请信应言简意赅，篇幅控制在一页之内，应说明申请人的资历优势，并有具体论据。态度要谦虚低调，自信大方，体现出申请人对该岗位或项目的重视；语言表述要易于阅读，体现个人风格。

2.4.4 格式规范（Standard Format）

关注细节，杜绝语法或拼写错误，给招聘或招生人员留下良好的第一印象。若知晓招聘或招生人员的姓名和头衔，应在申请信的开头部分直接称呼，以显示诚意与重视。

写作实践 Writing Tasks

▶▶ **Writing Practice 1**

Suppose you intend to apply for the position of sales assistant in a company. Please write an application letter to the manager of the company.

The job descriptions are as follows.

1) Responsibility: Responsible for the local management of marketing and sales

2) Requirements:

College degree and above

Basic familiarity with sales and marketing

English proficiency

Good communication and coordination skills

Work experience in international organizations is preferred.

▶▶ **Writing Practice 2**

Suppose you are an English major from a university in Xi'an and plan to apply for the graduate program at University of California, Los Angeles, to study English Language and Literature after graduation. Please write an application letter for admission. The self-introduction below is

for your reference.

　　×××，×××大学英文学院本科生，即将于2024年毕业，获文学学士学位。期间修读《高级英语》《学术英语写作》《英美文学》《西方文学理论》等课程，专业排名第3名，两次获校级奖学金一等奖。担任学院学生会副主席、班级班长，积极参加学校和院系活动，曾获2021年"外研社·国才杯"（"FLTRP·ETIC Cup"）全国英语写作大赛陕西省一等奖、2022年全国大学生英语竞赛陕西省特等奖。擅长文字工作，曾担任《×××大学学报》编辑部实习编辑。

第 3 单元　推荐信
Unit 3　Recommendation Letter

学习目标 Learning Objectives

1. 巩固掌握英文正式信函的格式；
2. 了解推荐信的特点与功能；
3. 掌握推荐信的主要构成部分与写作要点。

课前任务 Pretask

巩固英文正式信函的格式特点，思考推荐信的功能和要点。阅读一篇推荐信，并思考其与申请信的异同点。

引言 Introduction

推荐信（recommendation letter/reference letter/letter of support）是一封正式信函，旨在以专家或知情人的身份证明某人的能力、资历、成就及个性特点，以支持或推荐他/她申请入学、求职或获得奖项、奖学金等。推荐信往往随简历一同附上，是申请入学高校、教育机构或求职时必须提供的文件之一，且推荐信的质量和写信人的身份有可能会影响被推荐人能否成功申请到学位、职位或获得奖学金。本单元主要介绍推荐信的特点与功能、主要构成部分及写作要点。

知识要点 Key Knowledge

3.1 推荐信的功能（Functions of a Recommendation Letter）

推荐信通常是求学或求职申请材料中的一部分，其目的是向招生/招聘人员介绍被推荐人的学习和工作背景、研究领域、优势特长、成就业绩及个性特点等，并通过说明被推荐人符合申请要求条件而向招生或招聘单位进行推荐。通常情况下，推荐信一般应出自申请人所在领域内具有较高资历、较大学术影响力或一定社会地位的人士，如专家、教授、校长等，或者曾经与申请人共事并熟悉其能力、业绩及个性的人员，如导师、班主任、辅导员、部门主管、同事等。推荐人对申请人应十分了解或至少有一定的了解，并做到客观、真实、可靠。

3.2 推荐信的内容（Contents of a Recommendation Letter）

推荐信通常包括三个部分内容：引言、正文和结论。

在引言中，推荐人应首先明确说明自己写信的目的、被推荐人的姓名及其预期申请的项目、职位或奖项。推荐人还应简要介绍自己的个人情况，说明本人与被推荐人的关系、相识的时间以及了解的程度等。

范例：

> To those who are concerned,
>
> I am a visiting scholar in Johnson College. I have been working with Ellen Tumanut for ten months, and observing her EAP Writing and Grammar Class for the past two semesters. I am pleased to provide a letter recommending her for the Lieberman Teaching Excellence Award, which I think she totally deserves.

这个范例涵盖了推荐人的写信意图、被推荐人的基本情况以及二者的关系等基本信息。

推荐信的正文一般可以由若干段落构成，包括被推荐人的学习或工作态度、科研与学术能力、分析和解决问题的能力、沟通合作能力、未来发展潜力、语言能力以及取得的学术成就和业绩等，可使用"a good mastery of language and knowledge" "be actively involved"或"proficient"等表达。推荐信中还可以提到被推荐人的沟通协调或组织能力以及个性特点等，如具有领导力（leadership）、团队意识（a team-oriented attitude），或具有分析能力（analytical）和创新性（innovative）等，并举出具体实例和细节，以增强证明被推荐人资格或能力的说服力。

范例：

> What Ellen impressed me first were her amazing personal characteristics as a gifted teacher. She is confident and elegant in her manner, patient with her students, and creative in approaching her classes. As a colleague, she also shows great willingness to help me develop my teaching plan, answer my questions related to the class, and give me valuable suggestions.

As far as I am concerned, during Ellen's teaching experience, she manages to perform to her best capacities. As a writer herself, she is able to give students inspiring guidance and advice when they write. She also encourages students to learn actively and independently. In her class, for example, she organizes a variety of activities to motivate students, such as peer review of the first drafts of their papers, peer teaching, group discussion and presentation, test corrections, etc. She knows how to balance being strict with her students and encouraging them in the nicest way.

Ellen has quite a lot of strengths; however, the two main strengths, from my observations, are her excellent teaching style and her wholehearted devotion to her teaching career and students. As a doctoral candidate in education, Ellen has a very high level of communication skills with her students. She could detect students' weaknesses and strengths and encourage them to put what they have learnt into practice. Ellen is never satisfied with what she has achieved. Instead, she constantly adjusts the content and organization of each lesson, ways of teaching, and even grading rubrics according to students' performance. She spends long hours grading students' papers. She is always pursuing the best way to evaluate students—but not the most convenient or easiest way for her—so that students can really get improved rather than just being tested.

在推荐信的最后一段，推荐人会对被推荐人作出一个整体的评价，主要涉及被推荐人适合该项目或职位的原因，以及被推荐人未来在个人和专业方面会取得的成就，能够对该招生学校或招聘单位做出的贡献等。

范例：

To sum up, Ellen has displayed all the qualities that make herself a successful and unique teacher. She has a pleasant personality to work well with both students and colleagues. She specializes in the area that she is teaching and is fully committed to her work. She has made great contributions to the college and her colleagues with her outstanding performance. Therefore, I highly recommend her for the Lieberman Teaching Excellence Award and firmly believe that she will be a perfect role model for those who dedicate themselves to the great career of teaching.

3.3 如何写出成功的推荐信（How Write a Successful Recommendation Letter）

首先，作为一种正式信函，推荐信必须使用标准格式，包括信头、信内地址、称呼语、正文、结束语和签名。常见的称呼语有"To Whom It May Concern""Dear Sir or Madam"或者"Dear Admission Committee"等。此外，推荐信有时也可以打印在带有抬头与信内地址的正式信纸上。

其次，推荐信的内容应当具体清楚、实事求是，既应对被推荐人的资历能力给予积极正面的介绍与评价，也不能为掩盖其弱点而刻意夸大吹捧，歪曲事实。有时甚至可适当提及被推荐人的明显短板或缺点，并强调被推荐人为克服缺点正在做的积极努力。

再次，推荐信中应注意尽量提供被推荐人与其所申请的项目或职位相关的信息，并使用具体的事例和数据等来增强说服力，避免涉及与申请人的申请目标没有直接关系的信息或细节。

最后，推荐信用词应准确恰当，不使用含糊或模棱两可的陈述，以避免由于不准确的表述或解释不当的评价而引起歧义，导致适得其反的效果。

写作实践 Writing Tasks

▶ **Writing Practice**

Suppose a student plans to apply for a scholarship of a foreign university, which requires the candidates to have excellent academic performance in his/her major and can play an exemplary leading role. As the academic advisor of the class, you are requested to write a letter of recommendation for him/her in combination with the characteristics of his/her major and other relevant requirements of scholarship application.

第 4 单元 个人陈述
Unit 4　Personal Statement

学习目标 Learning Objectives

1. 了解个人陈述的特点与功能；
2. 掌握个人陈述的主要构成部分与写作要点；
3. 了解个人陈述与申请信的区别。

课前任务 Pretask

熟悉个人陈述的功能和目的，阅读一篇个人陈述，思考其内容中的特别之处，并指出其与申请信的区别。

引言 Introduction

个人陈述（personal statement）一般多用于申请海外留学，尤其是申请高校的研究生院或博士后研究职位等，是与个人简历、申请信等材料一并递交的申请文件（application package）中的一部分。个人陈述也是一份自我介绍，包含对自己个人经历的记叙和描述，以此向招生学校或招聘单位展示自己，因此也是最重要的申请材料之一。本单元主要介绍个人陈述的特点与功能、主要构成部分及写作要点。

知识要点 Key Knowledge

4.1　个人陈述的功能（Functions of Personal Statement）

个人陈述在英文中也可表述为 statement of purpose 或 personal essay，目的是向招生学校或招聘单位介绍申请人的背景、申请动机、学术能力、兴趣领域和工作或实习经历等。因此，申请人需要认真深入地思考个人的资历与闪光点、能够胜任所申请项目的原因，以及该项目的重要性等。申请人应该在个人陈述中展示自己独特的个性、经历和资历，能够引起招生/招聘部门的注意。

4.2 个人陈述的类型（Styles of Personal Statement）

根据申请高校或专业的不同，个人陈述一般可分为两种类型：综合概括型和回答问题型。

4.2.1 综合概括型（General and Comprehensive）

该类型的个人陈述对内容、覆盖范围、要点等均没有具体特别的要求，申请人可以根据个人实际情况突出个人的闪光点。

4.2.2 回答问题型（Response to Specific Questions）

在一些高校或研究院所要求提供的申请文件中，可能会包括一个申请表格，列出向申请人提出的一些问题。因此，申请人的个人陈述可以围绕这些问题展开，作为对其的回应，以有针对性地提供信息。

4.3 个人陈述的特点（Features of Personal Statement）

结合其功能及类型不难看出，虽然个人陈述也属于自我介绍，但无论在格式上还是内容上，与求职信或简历均有所不同，总体而言具有以下特征。

4.3.1 针对性（Targeted）

正如上文所说，个人陈述有时会包含申请表格，但表格中涉及的问题既有类似也有不同。申请人应针对表格中的问题，同时结合所申请机构及专业方向的特点提供针对性和个性化的回答。切忌千篇一律，更不能向同时申请的几所学校递交同一份个人陈述。

4.3.2 自荐性（Self-recommending）

个人陈述的功能与求职信及简历相似，其最根本的特点是自我推荐，以获得心仪的工作岗位或入学资格。因此，在个人陈述中既应实事求是地介绍个人情况，更要针对申请目的呈现申请人的优势特长，以证明自己具有足够强的学习和工作能力。

4.3.3 独特性（Unique）

在展示个人情况的过程中，申请人应采用充满独特性、个性化、新颖生动的表述，介绍自己的个性特征、研究领域及兴趣特长等，并强调个人经历中较为独特或能够更好体现个人能力与素质的内容，真正打动招生或招聘单位，给人留下良好印象。

4.4 个人陈述的结构（Structure of Personal Statement）

尽管不同单位或机构的要求可能有所区别，但个人陈述的格式与结构与常见的五段式文章类似，包括三个主要部分：引言、正文和结论，每个部分各有侧重。

4.4.1 引言（Introduction）

和一般的写作一样，个人陈述中引言部分的主要目的是吸引读者的注意，激发招聘或招生单位进一步了解申请人的兴趣。有很多方法可以帮助申请人实现这一目标：阐述申请人获取所申请项目信息的渠道或推荐人；介绍申请人目前所攻读的学位或所处的职位；表达申请人对所申请项目的热情或浓厚兴趣等。

关于个人兴趣的常见表达有：

- I have cherished the constant aspiration of becoming a chemist.
- I have much interest in the AI industry.
- That amazing trip marked the turning point in my life, and with it I commenced my quest for answers capable of unraveling those mysteries in nature.

4.4.2 正文（Body）

个人陈述的正文部分通常由几个各有侧重的段落组成，涵盖申请人对专业领域的浓厚兴趣、已掌握的专业知识以及专业学习的突出优势或经验，并在每个段落中辅以具体解释与支撑论据，以更好地彰显申请人的优势或个性。个人陈述的正文部分通常包括三个主体段落。

第一个主体段落主要是对申请人教育背景的简要概述，包括目前就读的大学、即将获得的学位、从事的专业及修读的课程等。第二个主体段落一般是对申请人在学术、研究和工作方面的介绍，尤其强调与该招生项目或招聘职位要求相符的知识、能力或资历，并在此基础上进一步说明申请该研究项目的原因。该部分可辅以过去曾获得的成果、奖项及其他形式的成就，结合未来研究兴趣和学业及职业规划目标，有力地证明申请人能够达到学习的目标和要求。第三个主体段落尽量说服用人单位接收该申请人。该部分可以详细阐述申请人所具有的资历以及未来职业规划，明确说明参加该项目或获得该职位能够帮助申请人实现的学业或职业目标。此外，申请人也可以强调其未来能对该项目或单位所做出的贡献。

需要注意的是，主体段落中的每个方面都应该结合具体实例，以确保说服力。此外，为了让该部分更具吸引力，获取招聘方的好感，申请人可以通过一到两个具体的案例，体现出自己不同寻常的个人经历或个性特点，如一次特殊意义的旅行、在某一特定领域所获得的奖项或成就等，以此说明申请人所具有的坚强性格或独特洞察力等。同时，个人陈述时也应考虑文本的统一性和连贯性这两个基本要素。统一性指所有主体段落都应当支撑引言部分所

提出的要点，且每个主体段落的开头都应有主题句，并列出细节加以论证；连贯性则指所有的主体段落应以一定的逻辑关系排列，每个段落中的前后句之间也应使用恰当的连接句或连接词，以便流畅、连贯地过渡思想。

主体部分的常见表达有：

- I am always fond of acquiring new knowledge and skills, which can inspire my creativity and innovation and facilitate me to quickly adapt to the fast-changing world.
- With a solid foundation in mathematics laid during senior middle school, I finally entered one of the most renowned universities to study it.
- Such a program will definitely enhance my expertise and broaden my perspectives.
- Due to my outstanding performance, I was selected to attend an international conference with local and international governmental bodies including the World Bank.

4.4.3 结论（Conclusion）

个人陈述的最后一部分是结论，对个人陈述的中心思想进行重述、强调并加以升华。因此，这一部分可简要重申上文中重点讨论的要点，并再次强调申请人的资历、经验、能力以及希望被录用的强烈愿望。最后，申请人可以表达一下决心和未来展望，给招聘人员留下深刻的印象。

常见的相关表达方式有：

- I believe that with the distinguished faculty and advanced facilities of your university, I will live up to my potential in both knowledge and experience.
- Famous for its exacting and nurturing academic atmosphere, your university is the one I have long admired.
- I hope that this will lay a foundation for my future academic research at some eminent research institutes or world-class companies.

4.5 如何写出成功的个人陈述（How Write a Successful Personal Statement）

结合以上内容不难看出，虽然申请信和个人陈述都是关于申请人的自我介绍，但二者之间仍然存在一些差别。申请信是正式信函的一种，具有特定的格式要求，且由于申请信往往和简历一同递交，可从简历中获得更多具体信息，因此申请信中对申请人的介绍往往较为简练。相反，个人陈述更像是一篇形式自由的文章，申请人在选择内容、主题、个人实例、特色和其他细节方面均有较大的发挥空间。简而言之，个人陈述的内容和形式比申请信丰富和灵活。但需要注意的是，无论是个人陈述还是申请信，都不应该冗长乏味，而应力争在最短的时间内迅速吸引招聘或招生人员的兴趣，给人留下良好而深刻的第一印象。

申请人若想在众多竞争对手中脱颖而出，个人陈述应具有以下因素：首先，即使有较大的灵活性，个人陈述的重点应包括申请理由，突出优势和独特个性；其次，个人陈述应用一定的篇幅说明申请人对所申请项目的重视度，并提供申请人能被录取的原因；再次，个人陈述的风格应当自然而得体，向招生或招聘人员展示申请人对语言的掌握程度和写作技巧，语气应真诚且自信，避免使用"杰出的（excellent）""了不起的（great）"等过于高调而又含糊的表达。

范例[1]：

> Originally I had been accepted to the University of Illinois at Urbana-Champaign's College of Business but financial pressures pushed me toward Parkland instead, a defining moment that proved to be the biggest business decision of my life. Despite my desire to spend all four years at UIUC, I realized that I could finish the equivalent of my first two years at Parkland for free, my first step toward long-term financial success. I knew that in order to handle the finances of others I needed to master my own and learn the ins and outs of money to lay down the foundation for my career. By taking charge of my personal finances first to begin my journey, it was clear to me that this external experience and immersion would prepare me to become a more qualified applicant than before, a better businessman.
>
> Through my studies in finance and accounting, I intend to become the CEO of my own company. Currently, I am running a tutoring business with 7 full-time students, in addition to my own full-time studies, for the second consecutive year and plan on doing so throughout my junior and senior years as well because I want to learn how to manage a company and gain perspective outside the classroom. Furthermore, I single-handedly resurrected the Business Club and Future Business Leaders of America-Phi Beta Lambda Chapter here at Parkland, boasting over 50 members. Together we are working with business students and MBA graduate Kerris Lee from the U of I on an extensive marketing campaign to bring more attention to Willard Airport, an initiative of former University of Illinois Chancellor Wise. By integrating my studies with these opportunities, I am confident that embracing the College of Business will provide me the experience necessary to succeed in the business world.

---

[1] 来自《谷歌学术》官方网站。

【解析】这份个人陈述详细介绍了申请人的个人背景、申请转学的动机、业绩成就和预期目标，结构清晰、组织合理、论述充分、表达流畅、清晰简洁，重点突出了申请人的资历优势和独特个性，能够赢得招聘人员的关注和青睐。

写作实践 Writing Tasks

▶▶ **Writing Practice**

Suppose you plan to apply for a graduate program in a university abroad. Please write the introductory paragraph of a personal statement based on your personal situation including your major, research field, future plan, etc.

第二部分　学术写作
Part 2　Academic Writing

内容提要
Preview

第二部分包括四个单元。其中，第 5 单元和第 6 单元介绍学术论文的框架和学术论文的语言风格，第 7 单元总结了学术英语写作中常用的技巧——直接引用、改写与总结，第 8 单元归纳了英语模糊限制语在学术英语写作中的用法。学习者可以通过这部分的讲练结合，在提高学术素养的同时，了解和掌握学术英语写作的特征与规范。

第 5 单元　学术论文的框架
Unit 5　Format of Academic Research Papers

学习目标 Learning Objectives
1. 了解英语学术论文的结构框架和七大要素；
2. 掌握英语学术论文中摘要、引言和文献综述的写作特点。

课前任务 Pretask
请找两三篇与你的专业相关的权威英语学术论文，仔细观察这几篇论文由哪几部分组成，比较一下其中参考文献的引用格式是否相同。

引言 Introduction
对学生来说，学术写作是素质教育和能力培养的重要组成部分。论文发表虽然是研究生毕业的必备条件，但论文写作，或是在本科期间发表论文，对以后的升学、就业都有非常大的帮助。因此，学术论文写作既是对学习生涯的总结和对所学专业知识的综合运用，也是学生形成初步科研能力的一种尝试，同时也有助于养成独立思考的习惯。学生可以通过英语学术论文写作熟悉学术论文的基本写作方法和写作规范，初步了解科研创作的一些基本技能，掌握文献资料检索的基本方法。英语学术论文写作的 IMRD（Introduction-Methods-Results-Discussion）框架模式在理工类的科技论文期刊中最为常见，即进行文献回顾、研究方法介绍、数据结果统计、研究意义挖掘等。本单元将介绍英语学术论文的结构框架和引用规范。

知识要点 Key Knowledge
英语学术论文的结构框架通常分为以下七个部分。

5.1 摘要（Abstract）

虽然摘要一般都是在论文的开头部分，但在实际写作中，作者会在正文完成之后再写摘要。摘要能够方便读者对论文进行检索和筛选，提升文献利用率。摘要是一篇研究型论文的简要总结，一般置于论文题名和作者之后，正文之前。摘要应说明论文的研究目的、研究问题、研究方法、研究结果和结论，重点一般是研究结果和结论。

摘要写作的注意事项：

（1）中文摘要一般不宜超过300字，英文摘要则不宜超过250个实词。

（2）平均句数9~10句，通常控制在10句以内。一般来说，研究背景介绍1~2句，研究方法介绍2~3句，主要结论5~6句。

（3）摘要中一般不用图表、化学结构式、非公知公用的符号和术语。

（4）摘要应具有独立性和自明性，即使读者在阅读全文之前，仅从摘要就能获得必要的信息。摘要不容赘言，内容须完整且具体，使人一目了然，但不必对论文内容做诠释和评论（尤其是不要做自我评价）。

（5）摘要不能脱离正文，更不能与论文内容相矛盾。不要引用在论文中没有提到的观点或研究，也不要把应在引言中出现的内容写入摘要。

（6）英文摘要不能只是对中文摘要的直接翻译，句子之间要上下连贯，互相呼应。慎用长句，句型结构应力求简单。每句话表意明白，无空泛、笼统、含糊之词。

（7）缩略语、简称、代号一般只有相关专业的读者能清楚理解，因此必须要在首次出现时加以说明。

请根据以上的摘要写作注意事项对比分析下面的两个摘要[1]。

Bad abstract:	Good abstract:
This paper will look at the human genome project and its goals. I will prove that scientists have ethical and moral questions about genetic engineering because of this project.	Begun in 1988, the human genome project intends to map the 23 chromosomes that provide the blueprint for the human species. The project has both scientific and ethical goals. The scientific goals underscore the advantages of the genome project, including identifying and curing diseases and enabling people to select the traits of their offspring, among other opportunities. Ethically, however, the project raises serious questions about the morality of genetic engineering. To handle both the medical opportunities and ethical dilemmas posed by the genome project, scientists need to develop a clear set of principles for genetic engineering and to continue educating the public about the genome project.

1　Carole. S. 1997. *Form and Style: Research Papers, Reports, Theses (Tenth Edition)*. Houghton Mifflin Harcourt.

范例[1]：

> ## Abstract
>
> The COVID-19 pandemic has created unprecedented burdens on people's physical health and subjective well-being. While countries worldwide have developed platforms to track the evolution of COVID-19 infections and deaths, frequent global measurements of affective states to gauge the emotional impacts of pandemic and related policy interventions remain scarce. Using 654 million geotagged social media posts in over 100 countries, covering 74% of world population, coupled with state-of-the-art natural language processing techniques, we develop a global dataset of expressed sentiment indices to track national—and subnational-level affective states on a daily basis. We present two motivating applications using data from the first wave of COVID-19 (from 1 January to 31 May 2020). First, using regression discontinuity design, we provide consistent evidence that COVID-19 outbreaks caused steep declines in expressed sentiment globally, followed by asymmetric, slower recoveries. Second, applying synthetic control methods, we find moderate to no effects of lockdown policies on expressed sentiment, with large heterogeneity across countries. This study shows how social media data, when coupled with machine learning techniques, can provide real-time measurements of affective states.

这是 Nature 上的一篇论文摘要，论文题目是 Global Evidence of Expressed Sentiment Alterations During the COVID-19 Pandemic，是关于新型冠状病毒疾病（Covid-19）流行期间情绪变化的全球证据的一则研究。摘要第 1、2 句介绍研究背景，指出 COVID-19 大流行给人们的身体健康和主观幸福感带来了前所未有的负担。虽然世界各国已经开发了平台来追踪 COVID-19 感染和死亡的演变，但频繁地用全球状态来衡量流行病和相关政策干预的情感影响仍然是稀缺的。句型 "… has created unprecedented burdens on…" 和 "… remain scarce" 阐述了研究背景和价值。第 3、4 句阐述了研究方法，这一部分主要使用了 "using…, covering…, coupled with…, we develop a global dataset of…" 和 "We present… using data from…" 来说明研究的样本选择和测量手段。第 5~7 句的句型 "we provide consistent evidence that…""…we find…""This study shows…" 展示了本文的两个研究结果。首先，COVID-19 爆发导致急剧下降的表达情绪，这种影响是不对称的；其次，各国的疫情封锁政策存在很大的差异。最后，这项研究表明，将社交媒体数据与机器学习技术相结合可以实时测量情感状态。

---

[1] Wang, J., Fan, Y. & Palacios, J. 2022. *Global Evidence of Expressed Sentiment Alterations During the COVID-19 Pandemic.* Nat Hum.

5.2 引言（Introduction）

引言不同于摘要，字数没有严格的限制，但内容要更加精准和明确。引言也可以成为绪论和导论，通常需要介绍研究背景、研究意义，该研究领域的发展状况、存在的局限性等，用于引出下文。引言是论文正文的第一部分。通过梳理研究背景有助于读者理解研究动机。作者要在引言部分先阐明研究主题，再综述相关文献，讨论现有研究的不足和局限性，引出研究问题，最后以研究目标结尾。引言的架构通常包括：

- 陈述研究背景、研究价值和意义；
- 指出该研究领域存在的问题、争议、局限性；
- 确定本篇论文的研究问题和研究目标；
- 对该领域之前的研究做一个概览和回顾，即文献回顾；
- 简要介绍本篇论文的工作和创新点；
- 总结性描述论文的结构。

范例[1]：

User Preferences Regarding Autonomous Vehicles

Introduction

Technological advances are influencing the way we travel. Autonomous vehicles (AVs) offer a unique solution to many of the current issues in transportation. They represent a technological leap forward that can influence how individuals view mobility (Howard & Dai, 2014). Autonomous vehicles offer a wide range of benefits, in terms of safety, efficiency, environmental impacts, and increased mobility.

The NHTSA estimates that human error is the main reason behind 90 percent of all crashes; AVs can likely eliminate the human error causes of vehicle crashes. Autonomous vehicles can provide efficiency benefits in terms of time efficiency, reduction in congestion, and efficient use of resources (KPMG, 2012). AVs allow "drivers" to free up the time traditionally spent monitoring the roadways, enabling them to use their time more effectively by sleeping, eating, relaxing, or working during the time traditionally spent driving. Vehicles currently spend

---

[1] Chana J. H. & Robert I. Y. S. 2017. *User Preferences Regarding Autonomous Vehicles*, Transportation Research Part C: Emerging Technologies.

over 90% of their lives parked and being unused (KPMG, 2012). AVs are able to reposition themselves, away from denser areas in order to enable development in land traditionally used for parking. The technology further enables the optimization of traffic flow management through the creation of platoons, thus potentially reducing overall congestion on the roadways and reducing fuel consumption and CO_2 emissions.

AVs can also impact travel-behavior, notably in the form of increased mobility for children, the elderly and the disabled who are not able to drive. However, this may cause negative effects as a result of increased road capacity demands and vehicle-miles travelled (VMT) (Fagnant and Kockelman, 2014, Fagnant and Kockelman, 2015).

One of the major advantages of AV technology is that it allows the creation of a new travel mode which is a hybrid between private and public modes and combines the advantages of both: communally-owned, shared vehicles. Ownership of private vehicles has been on the rise since the invention of the automobile. However, the lack of affordability of privately owned vehicles and the lack of comparable transportation options has led to the creation of shared vehicle systems. The development of fully self-driving cars will solve many of the barriers associated with shared vehicle systems, from both the providers' and users' perspective and enhance the systems. These include repositioning vehicles to better service demand and improving users' ability to access the vehicles. Despite the advantages, individuals are often hesitant to embrace new technology. This paper aims to better understand who will use autonomous vehicles under various scenarios and to gain insight into these hesitations and how to overcome them. Individual attitudes regarding AVs are important since the public controls the demand for the technology, governing policies and future investments in infrastructure. This study models users' preference regarding the adoption of AVs with distinction between shared and owned vehicles. Characteristics of the individual (socioeconomic characteristic, attitudes and behaviors, and current travel behavior) and characteristics of the system (ownership, control, costs and parking supply) are among the factors hypothesized to influence the decision to purchase and use private autonomous vehicles (PAVs) and shared autonomous vehicles (SAVs). An additional objective is to examine the differences in AV preference for vehicle type between individuals in Israel and in North America.

5.3 文献综述（Literature Review）

  文献综述也称文献回顾，主要是通过梳理某一个学科领域中已有的文献，总结这个领域的研究现状，从现有文献及过去的学术研究成果中，发现需要进一步研究的问题和角度。撰写文献综述看似简单，其实是一项高难度的工作。作者要就某一领域的某一方面的课题或研究专题搜集大量资料，综合分析当前该课题或研究专题的最新进展、学术见解和建议，从而揭示研究的新动态、新趋势、新水平、新原理和新技术等，为后续研究寻找出发点、立足点和突破口。文献综述是科学研究和论文的一个重要组成部分，好的文献综述可以提高研究的可信度。它向读者展示论文作者对该研究领域的了解程度，为研究提供了理论依据和理论框架。写文献综述时一个普遍容易犯的错误是，把研究主题相关的概念、术语、理论和背景介绍等同于文献综述，有的作者习惯将文献综述写进引言的部分，但文献综述通常是独立的部分。

  文献综述通常有三种顺序：时间顺序、主题顺序和方法论顺序。其中，时间顺序（chronological order）是将文献按发表的时间顺序来整理述评；主题顺序（thematic order）则是根据该研究背景的主题分类，针对每一类的主题研究进行分别述评；方法论顺序（methodological order）是按照该研究主题的文献中所采取的不同的研究方法进行分类，然后再进行分别述评。

  另外，在写英文文献综述时，应注意动词时态。文献综述通常采用三种时态：过去时、现在时和现在完成时。如果述评的重点是讨论研究本身或具体的某位研究者，那么最好使用一般过去时，这是文献综述最常用的时态。应将该研究主题作为句子主语，如"Jones (2013) reported that…"。如果所引述的是相对比较久远的观点、发现或者结论时，通常使用一般现在时（也有作者喜欢使用一般过去时），通常这样的文献对现在的研究仍有较大影响，如"Dewey's philosophy of education is that an experience-based curriculum promotes more effective learning and a greater competence in living."；如果引述的文献研究是近来发表的，可以使用现在完成时，如"Recent studies have demonstrated that… (Jones, 2015; Pinto 2014.)"；也可以用现在完成时来概括某个领域过去的研究，如"Several researchers have studied these stimuli…"。

  文献综述是对一定时期内某一学科或某一研究专题的学术成果和研究进展进行系统、全面地概述和评论，可以体现作者整合（synthesize）、归纳（summarize）、分析（analyze）、转述（paraphrase）等能力。

范例[1]:

Does organized sports participation in childhood and adolescence positively influence health? A review of reviews

Literature Review

Regular participation in physical activity (PA) is associated with several physical and mental health benefits. Based on extensive research, PA recommendations have been developed, entailing at least 60 min per day of moderate-to-vigorous intensity physical activity (MVPA) for children and adolescents aged 5–17 years (World Health Organization, 2010). Complying with these recommendations is associated with increased physical fitness, reduced body fat, favorable cardiovascular and metabolic disease risk profiles, enhanced bone health, and reduced symptoms of depression and anxiety (Physical Activity Guidelines Advisory Committee, 2018; World Health Organization, 2010). Nevertheless, it has been estimated that about 80% of young persons (aged 11–17) globally do not meet the recommended minimum of 60 min of MVPA daily (Sallis et al., 2016).

The concept of PA incorporates a great diversity of activities including domestic, occupational, transport, and leisure-time contexts, the latter of which comprises physical exercise, sport, and unstructured recreation. Sport is commonly defined as being organized, and is usually competitive and played in a team or as an individual (Khan et al., 2012). Organized sport is one of the most popular forms of leisure-time activities worldwide, with at least one-third of children and adolescents participating in most countries (Aubert et al., 2018). Moreover, sports participation and access to sport/recreational facilities are consistently reported as correlated with PA in the literature (Sterdt et al., 2014). Participation is much higher in high-income countries, with yearly participation rates between 60% and 80% (Aubert et al., 2018), whereas there is still uncertainty concerning equal and affordable sports participation opportunities within, and between countries (Aubert et al., 2018).

The European Union (EU) White Paper on sports policy claims that EU sports policy should be evidence based (European Union, 2014). A linkage between organized sports

---

1 Helga B. B., Thomas W. & Ellen S. 2021. *Does Organized Sports Participation in Childhood and Adolescence Positively Influence Health?* Preventive Medicine Reports.

participation and health-enhancing PA is assumed and warranted, and the EU also focuses on safeguarding children's rights in sports, and guidelines for gender equality. To further support healthy and evidence-based sports and sports policy development, the highest level of evidence concerning the relation between participation in organized sports and health needs to be examined and reported.

Organized sports participation is associated with higher levels of PA, favorable motor development, and healthier eating habits (Nelson et al., 2011), whereas the potentially beneficial effects on weight development, bone health, cardiometabolic health, and psychosocial health are less well documented (Venetsanou et al., 2015). Furthermore, positive associations with psychological and social health factors have been reported (Clark et al., 2015; Mansfield et al., 2018), while potentially negative effects include increased consumption of alcohol and smokeless tobacco, and higher levels of stress, maltreatment, burnout, eating disorders, and overuse injuries (Bean et al., 2014; Vella, 2019). Overuse injuries and negative weight control are typically accentuated by early specialization, large amounts of practice, and a negative motivational climate (Bean et al., 2014).

Based on the abovementioned reviews, sports participation might have the potential for both positive and negative health outcomes. The evidence summarized above relies on combinations of experimental, longitudinal, and cross-sectional primary studies (Bean et al., 2014; Clark et al., 2015; Diehl et al., 2012; Kwan et al., 2014; Mansfield et al., 2018; Nelson et al., 2011; Vella, 2019; Venetsanou et al., 2015), with consequences for the strength of evidence concerning causal relationships between sports participation and health. Cultural contexts and differences, types of sports, and age as well as gender, could also possibly alter positive and negative associations between organized sports and health (Eime et al., 2013a, 2010, 2013b). Over the past two decades, the number of published systematic reviews has increased markedly, which can be confirmed by a rapid database search. Hence, the logical next step would be to systematically conduct reviews of existing systematic reviews, to provide decision makers in public health and sports policy as well as future research studies with the required evidence.

5.4 研究方法（Methods）

任何一项研究都离不开研究方法的支撑。研究方法一般包括文献调查法、观察法、文献研究法、实证研究法、实验法等。论文的研究方法部分是对应用于该研究的系统性和理论性方法的分析，描述了这篇论文是如何进行研究的，以及选择这种研究方法的原因。

范例[1]：

Methods

Participants and procedure

Participants were people older than 18 years living in Spain and experiencing the required (mandatory) situation of lock-down at home, beginning on Monday 16th of March after the government's decision. Participation in this study was requested through social networks and all the options available for the researchers to contact potential participants. The same description and request for participation was sent to associations or institutions that frequently collaborate with the research team, as well as to other potential associations or institutions contacted through social networks such as Whatsapp, Facebook or Linkedin. The data presented here were gathered from Saturday 21st of March (at 19:00 hours) to Thursday 24th of March (at 21:00 hours). All participants provided their consent to participate in the study and during the first week of lock-down answered a survey that was developed using Google Forms. The study was approved by the Ethics Committee of the Hospital Universitario Fundación Alcorcón.

Measures

In addition to age, gender, and marital status, self-perceptions of aging were measured through the same procedure used by Levy, Slade, Kunkel and Kasl (2002), with the Liang and Bollen (1983) Attitudes Toward Own Aging subscale. This is a 5-item scale (e.g., "Things keep getting worse as I get older"), with higher scores indicating more negative selfperceptions of aging. Cronbach's alpha of this scale in the current sample was 0.60.

Stressors. Considering sources of stress that have been identified as related with COVID-19, such as the risk to clinicians' physical health (Dewey, Hingle, & Linzer, 2020), fear about own health (Brooks et al., 2020), and massive quantities of information about the pandemic Accepted Manuscript 6 (Van Bavel et al., 2020), the following questions were included: "Do you have a profession or vital situation that puts you in a risk situation?" (Answers:

---

1 Losada-Baltar. 2021. *"We Are Staying at Home." Association of Self-perceptions of Aging, Personal and Family Resources, and Loneliness with Psychological Distress during the Lock-Down Period of COVID-19*. Journal of Gerontology Series B-Psychological Sciences and Social Sciences.

"no" and "yes") and "Do you consider yourself to be at risk of serious health outcomes if getting COVID-19?" (Answers: "no" "yes", and "I don't know."). The item "How much time do you devote to looking for and processing information related to COVID-19 and the current situation? (e.g., news, radio or TV, Internet, others)" was included. (Answers range from 0 "not at all" to 10 "I am attentive to all the possible information.")

Family resources. The items "I am satisfied with the support that I receive from my family" (adapted from the APGAR questionnaire (Smilkstein, 1978), with answers ranging from 0 "almost never" to 2 "always"), "I feel that I am a burden to my family" (from the Self-Perceived Burden Scale (Cousineau et al., 2003); answers from 0 "never or almost never" to 4 "almost always"), and "How much contact do you have with relatives different to those you reside with?" (Answers range from 0 "no contact at all" to 10 "I have all the contact that I need.") were included. In addition, participants were requested to report how many people (different from themselves) they were co-residing with.

Personal resources. Ad hoc questions were included to measure diverse personal resources related with emotion regulation, behavioral, cognitive and social coping strategies selected among the many and diverse potential resource variables analyzed in the stress and coping literature. Specifically, questions were included to measure daily positive emotions ("How many moments of happiness, humor, laughter, or positive emotions do you have per day?"; answers from 0 "no moment at all" to 10 "I have many moments per day."); entertainment resources ("To what extent do you feel that you have resources for entertaining yourself at home?"; Answers from 0 "I have nothing to entertain myself with." to 10 "I have all the things I need."); and self-efficacy ("To what extent do you feel capable of coping effectively with the current situation?"; answers from 0 "not at all capable" to 10 "totally capable"). Daily Accepted Manuscript 7 time devoted to exercise was reported in a scale from 0 "no time at all" to 4 "more than one hour and a half"). Quality of sleep was rated in a scale ranging from 0 "very bad" to 3 "very good". Finally, as an indicator of expressed emotion, the following items based on the Family Attitude Scale (Kavanagh et al., 1997) were included: "To what extent do you like to have people around?", "I feel that people living with me are driving me crazy." "I lose my temper with those living with me.", and "I shout at people living with me." Cronbach's alpha for these 4 items in this sample is 0.87.

Loneliness. Perceived loneliness was measured using the same procedure as Kool and Geenen (2012), through the item "How much loneliness do you feel?" with answers ranging from 0 "I do not feel lonely at all." to 10 "I feel absolutely lonely."

Psychological distress. A wide array of psychological responses to COVID-19 have been described, including anxiety and depression (Wang et al., 2020), anger or fear (Brooks et al., 2020). With the aim of providing a brief measure of these diverse emotions, and drawing on research providing support for the use of single-item measures of emotional problems (e.g., Zimmerman et al., 2006), an ad-hoc 5-item scale was developed that measured, respectively, anxiety, anger, sadness, fear and hope (e.g., "How much sadness do you feel"). Answers ranged from 0 "I do not feel _____ at all." to 10 "I feel totally _____.", except for the item measuring hope, which was reversed. Cronbach's alpha for this scale with the current sample is 0.80.

Data analysis

In addition to descriptive and correlational analyses, two hierarchical regression analyses were conducted to examine the association between the assessed variables and loneliness and psychological distress, using the SPSS software (Version 22.0). Drawing upon the stress and Accepted Manuscript 8 coping model, sociodemographic variables were included in the first step, followed by stressors, family resources, personal resources, and loneliness.

作者在本研究中对1,310名处于新冠隔离期的西班牙人（年龄：18~88岁）进行问卷调查。问卷包括了参与者对新型冠状病毒疾病具体问题的回答，测量了家庭和个人资源、孤独感和心理困扰的自我认知，采用分层回归分析方法评估孤独感与心理痛苦的相关性。作者用"participants、…was measured、…analyses were conducted to examine…、using the SPSS software (Version 22.0)"等词和句型引出对研究方法的具体描述。研究方法范例采用的是调查法，二级标题包括Participants、Procedure、Data analysis等。如果是用实验法，那么二级标题一般包括Equipments and hardware、Materials、Procedure、Data analysis，介绍实验数据的收集和分析过程。

研究方法部分常用的句型有：

- Seven questions, adapted from X, assessed…
- All survey questions utilized a 5-point Likert scale.
- Using a 5-point Likert scale, participants were asked…

- The first step in this process was to…
- In the follow-up phase of the study, participants were asked…
- The final stage of the study comprised a semi-structured interview with participants who…
- Comparisons between the two groups were made using unrelated t-tests.
- 15 subjects were recruited using email advertisements requesting healthy students from…
- To control for bias, measurements were carried out by another person.
- To assess whether and how Xs are produced and received, we measured…
- The cohort was divided into two groups according to…
- A systematic literature review was conducted of studies that…
- Just over half the sample (53%) was female, of whom 69% were…
- Of the initial cohort of 123 students, 66 were female and 57 male.

5.5 研究结果（Results）

研究结果是一篇论文真正的重点和核心，一般放在论文的第三部分，但有些期刊论文中的研究结果与研究讨论会放在同一部分。研究结果主要是回答一个基本的问题："研究发现了什么？"它主要报告研究的实验数据，强调关键发现，并对数据进行概括性的比较。研究结果要解释作者的研究发现，常常用图表和定量数据等展示研究结果。图表和图解具有自明性，与文字是互为补充的，每个图表和图解都应有编号和标题。

范例：

Results 1[1]

23 studies were included in this review. The included interventions targeted various areas of mental health including depression, anxiety, overall wellbeing, and mental health awareness. The interventions were commonly delivered through mobile apps, web-based apps, and desktop apps. In addition, we explore design methodologies applied in the development of the interventions: we note significant stakeholder engagement in the studies, the inclusion of multiple stakeholder types (students, health care professionals, university staff, and young people in the general population), and limited use of design frameworks. Finally, in exploring

---

[1] Olugbenga O. & Ian P. 2021. *Online Mental Health Interventions Designed for Students in Higher Education: A User-centered Perspective.* Internet Interventions.

> user engagement, attrition rates and user acceptance, we find that most of the studies have not progressed enough (i.e., at pilot/prototype stages of development) to determine the impact of design methodologies on the success of these interventions.
>
> **Results 2**[1]
>
> In total, 58 longitudinal studies met the inclusion criteria and were synthesized in the review. We found that higher sedentary behavior among children and adolescents was associated with increased depression, anxiety and other mental health problems later in life. A dose-response association between sedentary behavior and mental health was observed, suggesting that children and adolescents who spend more time on SB may have a higher risk of developing poorer mental health later.

这部分应将研究成果有逻辑地、客观地按照一定顺序列出，将研究的实验或调查数据用清晰明了的方式让读者了解。这部分一般使用现在时，可以用一些常用的转述性动词（如show、reveal、betray、indicate、suggest、describe 等）引出研究结果。

常用的转述性动词：

(1) Verbs and other expressions neutral in meaning: according to, comment, describe, note, state, acknowledge, define, discuss, point out

(2) Verbs that indicate the author's position on an issue: argue, claim, emphasize, recommend, suggest, assert, defend, maintain, reject, support, challenge, doubt, put forward, refute

(3) Verbs that indicate what the author's thinking: assume, consider, recognize, believe, hypothesize, think

(4) Verbs that indicate that the author is showing something: demonstrate, illustrate, present, explain, indicate, show

(5) Verbs that indicate that the author is proving something: confirm, prove, validate, establish, substantiate, verify

(6) Verbs that indicate what the author did: analyze, estimate, examine, investigate, study, apply, evaluate, find, observe

---

[1] Jing Z., Shu X. Y. & Liang W. 2022. *The Influence of Sedentary Behaviour on Mental Health Among Children and Adolescents: A Systematic Review and Meta-analysis of Longitudinal Studies.* Journal of Affective Disorders.

5.6 讨论/结论（Discussion）

这部分主要讨论研究发现或研究结果的意义。作者会在讨论/结论部分回应在论文开头提出的研究问题，讨论前文所提出的研究假设（hypothesis），阐明前人在这个领域里所做的研究的关系、异同及不足之处。在引述前人研究的时候，须阐明对前人的研究成果做出的修改（modify）、补充（complement）、证实（prove）或者否定（deny）。讨论/结论部分要对研究结果以及可能影响到研究结果的因素进行解释，如果研究设计有多个因素和变量，还可以分别进行讨论。

这部分常用的句型有：

（1）讨论前文提出的研究假设（discussing hypothesis）

- The research investigated the differences between…/The results (data) show that…/The possible reason is…
- The aim of the research was to…/In the present study, it was found that… because…
- This study attempted to investigate… However, the findings show that…/It is found that… results in…
- It was originally assumed that…/The result show…/This suggests that…
- Existing theories suggested that…/The results, however, show…/This evidence led us to infer that… Thus, …

（2）进一步解释说明研究结果（explaining results）

- One reason for this could be that inadequate use of… increased…
- It is possible that an erroneous value was attributed to (due to)…
- It may be that the error in Equation caused the inaccuracy of…
- This inaccuracy seems to show that the materials used are…

（3）表示推断或结论（giving implications or conclusions）

- These results indicate/suggest/show/imply that…
- The data reported here imply/confirm that…
- Our conclusion is that…
- Therefore we may infer that…
- These findings support the hypothesis that…

- It appears/seems/suggests that…
- Our data provide the evidence that…

（4）表示本研究的局限性或不足之处（pointing out limitations）

- The proposed model in this study is based on the…
- Our analysis neglects several potential important conditions.
- The method of the research design is accurate, but cannot be implemented in real time applications.
- Only three groups of samples were tested.
- An experiment employing different TM Scanning approaches might produce different results.
- We recognized that the method adopted here does not cover the variety and complexity of melting rate…
- We readily admit that… may not fully identify…

（5）对未来研究方向和内容的建议（giving recommendations or solutions）

- Further research could explore the possibility to apply…
- A further experiment should be conducted with…
- In the future, the effect of… will be examined.
- Another interesting topic would be to examine how…
- An important direction for further work might be…
- The results in the study may lead to the development of effective methods for…
- In the future, we will investigate the …
- Researchers of this paper are now conducting experiments with …
- We suggest/ recommend that …

5.7 参考文献（References）

学术论文的参考文献是一个重要的部分。不管是对学术观点的立证，还是对文献综述的回顾，以及对经验证据的理论分析，都需要一定文献资料的支撑，这样才会使论文更具有说服力和科学性。因此，所有论文的结尾都要附有参考文献。在论文撰写过程中，正确引用

(5) However, most research on academic dishonesty has relied primarily on self-reports of cheating behaviors.

Function: _____

(6) The wide gap between the women's expressed opinion about infant-feeding and what they actually practiced is further underscored by the data in Table 8.

Function: _____

(7) Since the discovery of X rays in 1895, ionizing radiation has been a part of our life and consciousness.

Function: _____

(8) The present survey was conducted to investigate the understanding of radiation phenomena and risk among Norwegians with a reasonable level of general education, but lacking specialization in physical science.

Function: _____

(9) Combined, these data show that students improved their knowledge of individual concepts and their understanding of the greenhouse effect and global warming phenomenon.

Function: _____

(10) The study sample comprised 558 randomly selected Nigerian women residents in Surulere.

Function: _____

▶▶ **Read the following abstract Analyze the research objective, methods, findings and implications.**

Abstract

The present research examines how the molecular weight of PAA affects its influence on the crystallization of $CaCo_3$. Factors of calcium concentration and temperature were monitored in heated supersaturated solutions containing PAA samples which raise the temperature necessary to induce crystallization. Testing of mixed molecular weight distributions demonstrated that high molecular weight species govern the observed inhibition influence. An equation was also developed for predicting the influence of a mixed molecular weight distribution on crystallization temperatures at unsaturated surface conditions, assuming each polymer species produces a specific crystallization temperature. The microstructure of these crystals indicates the roughness results from the aligned aggregation of crystallites on the surface of existing crystals in a process that resembles a form of self-assembly.

▶▶ **Find an academic research article in your discipline or major. Analyze the Introduction section and Literature Review section. Find out the sentences in the two sections that are related to the following ideas.**

(1) Topic of the present research

(2) Significance of the present research

(3) Description of the previous studies

(4) Gap / limitations of the previous studies

(5) Purpose of the present research

(6) Research methodology of the present research

第6单元　学术文体风格
Unit 6　Academic Style

🎯 学习目标 Learning Objectives

1. 了解学术英语的概念和学术英语文体风格；
2. 掌握学术英语写作的主要特点和技巧。

课前任务 Pretask

什么是学术文体风格呢？比较下列几组句子，判断每组中哪句话更符合学术英语文体风格。

Group 1:
- In addition, inflation is an important factor.
- And inflation is an important factor.

Group 2:
- Russell (2001) states that over 50% of the population are unaware of the problem.
- Everybody knows that most people are unaware of the problem.
- Most people are unaware of the problem.

Group 3:
- The turning point was in the late 1980s.
- The turning point was about 30 years ago.

Group 4:
- In the experiment, the water was heated…
- In the experiment, I heated the water…

Group 5:
- There were four main reasons for the decline.
- What were the reasons for the decline?

Group 6:

- The increasing pollution of the environment is a global concern.
- The environment is increasingly polluted. This is a global concern.

引言 Introduction

怎样写出一篇具有学术风格的论文？如果在学术英语写作中带着日常生活中的口语体，显然是不符合学术写作风格的。本单元主要介绍学术英语写作的一些文体特征。

知识要点 Key Knowledge

英语按不同分类可分为一般生活英语、专业英语和学术英语等。其中，专业英语（Specialty English）是指专业性很强的英语，在某领域有规范用法，如法律英语、计算机英语等；学术英语（Academic English）一般是科研人员在研究过程中用到的英语。

请看下列例句和词语，比较生活英语、专业英语和学术英语的区别：

- May I take your order?
- Cheating and plagiarism will not be tolerated in any sense.
- At a grand gathering on Feburary 25, President Xi announced China's "complete victory" in its fight against absolute poverty.
- Clean up your room.
- Gravitational radiation.
- There are four basic tests required for transistors in practical applications: gain, leakage, breakdown, and switching time.
- Thermodynamics.

生活英语是口语化的，人们可以在旅行、购物、日常交流等场景下使用，对熟练程度没有要求。专业英语和学术英语的侧重点不同、范围不同、对象不同。专业英语的专业性表现在：专业词汇、专业的表达方式、约定俗成的专业规范；学术英语一般用于研究界与学术界，如学术期刊的论文、学术演讲或报告。英语母语者也必须学习学术英语，因为学术英语和生活英语大不相同。下面这篇文章节选自一篇学术英语论文，请从中找出学术写作的主要特点。

范例[1]:

Chinese Voices: Chinese Learners and Their Experiences of Studying in the UK

Chinese students have an increasingly high profile in UK universities. In 2005 the number of Chinese students in UK universities was put at 50,000 (Higher Education Statistics Agency, 2007). According to Universities and Colleges Admissions Service (UCAS) (UCAS, 2008) nearly 5,000 Chinese students were accepted to start courses at British universities in Autumn 2008, a rise of 14.7% on 2007. However, demographic changes in China and increasing competition from other parts of the globe offering higher education courses mean that the number of students is expected to peak in 2011 (Gill, 2008). As more institutions seek to attract a dwindling number of students we can expect greater competition between universities and a resulting increase in the interest of the student experience. It is vital that institutions listen carefully to the experiences that their Chinese students are living through if they are to continue to attract students in the face of worldwide competition.

Finances aside, simply by virtue of the number of Chinese students in UK universities, the Chinese student voice needs to be heard so we can be sure they are receiving the same opportunities as other students in the university system. Indeed "understanding overseas" students concerns and problems is essential for institutions in counseling, helping their overseas students, and in improving the quality of their services (Li & Kaye, 1998).

This research employed qualitative research methodology to give a voice to Chinese students whose transcribed experiences are presented in this paper. Specifically the research attempted to answer these questions:

① What are the main characteristics of the Chinese learner and the Chinese education system?

② What experiences do Chinese students have of living in the UK?

③ What experiences do Chinese students have of studying in the UK?

---

1 Mcmahon A. P. 2011. *Chinese Voices: Chinese Learners and Their Experiences of Living and Studying in the United Kingdom*. Journal of Higher Education Policy and Management.

通过范例可以发现学术英语的一些语言特点：

- 使用正式的学术语言，避免口语化；
- 多以第三人称进行写作，常使用非人称的结构（impersonal structure）；
- 具有客观性和公正性；
- 通常使用被动语态；
- 用词严谨；
- 正确规范的引用；
- 文章结构清晰；
- 段落常以主题句开头；
- 较多使用连接词。

掌握以下技巧，可以让学术英语写作更正式，更规范。

1. 避免使用第一/二人称代词

第一人称代词（I、we）和第二人称代词（you）会使文章看起来过于个人化且不正式，抑或口语化。但如果表达的是明确的个人观点，或者是作者希望与读者建立直接关系，也可以适当使用第一/二人称代词。比较下面两个句子：

例 1：I have divided the participants into three groups according to their study habit differences.

例 2：The participants are divided into three groups according to their study habit differences.

可以看出，未使用人称代词的例 2 更客观、更正式。

2. 避免使用英文缩写

避免使用英文缩略式，如 it's、don't、you're、shouldn't，这些是非正式写作风格，在学术英语写作应该避免这种缩略式。

3. 注意用词及语言表达的准确性

避免使用模糊且笼统的词语或表达方式，如 lots of、like、thing，应该使用如 a significant proportion of、a considerable number of、such as、factor、issue 或 topic。避免使用 every、all、none、nothing、best 和 worst 这类词，因为这些词很难去证明它的真实性。例如，最好不要写这样的句子："Everybody agrees that health care should be free." 相反，应该写成："Surveys of public opinion indicate a strong belief that health care should be free." 另外，在学术英语写作中，为了精确和可靠，数字的使用居多。例如：

Chemists had attempted to synthesize quinine for the previous hundred years but all they had achieved was to discover the extreme complexity of the problem. The volatile oily liquid beta-chloro-beta-ethyl sulphide was first synthesized in 1854, and in 1887 it was reported to produce blisters if it touched the skin. It was called mustard gas and was used at Ypres in 1917, when it caused many thousands of casualties.

由此可见，当你可以使用"50 million people"的时候，就尽量避免使用"a lot of people"这种笼统的表达。

4. 避免带有强烈个人情感色彩的形容词和副词

避免使用个人化和情绪化的表达语，如 luckily、remarkably、surprisingly、terrible、ridiculous 和 devastating，因为这些词会影响语气，使文章像新闻报道一样跌宕起伏；相反，客观的语言风格更有助于学术交流。比较一下：

例1：The low family income speeds up the *terrible* change in infant-feeding practice.

例2：The low family income speeds up the *negative* change in infant-feeding practice.

可以看到，例2把形容词"terrible"改成了"negative"，使句子读起来不那么耸人听闻，更为正式。

5. 避免使用修辞性的问句

学术英语写作中的修辞性问句（rhetorical questions）不符合学术英语的写作习惯。例如，"Is the British tax system good or not?"并不是在询问，而是在暗示或引出观点。因此，更正式、更客观的英文表达应该是："It is important to consider the effectiveness of the British tax system."

6. 避免过多使用短语动词

下面是一些常见的短语动词及其同义词。

	bring along	bring
	start again	resume, recommence
	go up	rise, increase
Phrasal verbs (verbs + prepositions or adverbs)	go down	fall, decrease
	find out	determine, discern, discover
	pick up	collect
	put in	insert
	fill out (a form)	complete

7. 较多地使用被动语态

被动句在学术写作中常用于两种情形：

第一，强调行动和结果，而不是动因；

第二，不用第一人称代词时。

例如：It is reported that the effect was not statistically significant. 这个被动句式会使句子读起来更客观。The way of classifying is based on the idea that an entire country is essentially rich or poor. 这个句子使用被动语态强调的是动作而不是动作的发起者。

8. 使用名词化现象较多

名词化（nominalization）是把动词或形容词（或其他词性）用作名词的语法现象。名词化在学术英语写作中很常见，可以渲染一种非个人化且客观的语气。

例 1：If we don't recognize the serious problem of growing population, we will make a big mistake.

例 2：Failure to recognize the seriousness of growing population will lead to a big mistake.

比较上面这两个句子你会发现，例 2 把某些动词和形容词改为了名词，增强了句义的多重性和表达的简洁性。

9. 注意学术词语的使用

学术写作中的正式词汇和专业词语拼写较长且较复杂，如 deteriorate、positive、negative 和 offspring，比 worse、good、bad 和 kids 这样的口语词汇更受青睐。我们可以使用基于学术词汇表（AWL）的词汇分析工具，检查英文写作中 AWL 的百分比。

写作实践 Writing Tasks

▶▶ Read the following sentences. Choose which parts of A, B, C or D are improper for academic use. Correct these parts to follow a formal writing style.

(1) And the resources are allocated to different places according to the needs.
　　 A　　　　　　　　　　　B　　　　　　　　C　　　　　　　　　　D

(2) Obviously better studying habits are needed, such as reading, reviewing and so on.
　　　　　　A　　　　　B　　　　　　C　　　　　　　　　　　　　　　D

(3) Volunteering social activities are wonderful experiences for children.
　　　　　A　　　　　　B　　　　　　C　　　　　　　　　　　D

(4) It is indicated that your physical conditions will be affected by this type of food.
　　　A　　　　　　　　B　　　　　　　C　　　　　　　　　D

(5) There are some different theories and some of them are OK to use.
　　　　　　　A　　　　　B　　　　　　　　C　　　　　　　D

(6) If the environment is not protected, our next generation will suffer the most.
　　　A　　　　　　　　　　B　　C　　　　　　　　　　　　　D

(7) But there are many restaurants where endangered animals are served.
　　A　　　　　　　B　　　　　　　　　　　　　　C　　　D

(8) The economic situation won't improve until efforts are made by the government.
　　　　　　　　A　　B　　　　　　　　C　　　　　　　D

(9) The fact that these women have positive attitudes towards breast feeding is surprising.
　　　A　　　　　　　　　　　B　　　　　　C　　　　　　　　　　　D

(10) There are many causes for students' exhaustion, such as poor diet, part-time jobs, etc.
　　　　　　　　　A　　　　B　　　　　　　　　　　　　　C　　　　　　　　D

第 7 单元　直接引用、改写与总结
Unit 7　Quoting, Paraphrasing and Summarizing

学习目标 Learning Objectives
1. 了解学术写作中规范引用的必要性，避免学术不端；
2. 掌握直接引用、改写和总结的引用方式。

课前任务 Pretask
仔细阅读一两篇研究主题相似的英文文献，做好笔记，用英语写下文献中的研究目的、方法、结果和结论等。

引言 Introduction
写作时往往需要将前人的研究观点纳入论文中，即引用。引用一般有三种方式：直接引用（quote）、改写（paraphrase）、总结（summarize）。不论是哪一种，都须使用符合学术规范的引用格式。正确的引用、改写和总结可以有效地避免抄袭，但必须注明参考来源。

知识要点 Key Knowledge

7.1　直接引用（Quote）
直接引用要在引用的原文前后加上引号，表明是直接使用了原文的表述。在论文写作中，直接引用的次数不宜过多，否则会影响研究的可信度和文章的相似度。所以，一篇论文

中直接引用的次数最好不要超过三次，长度也不要超过两句话。

7.2 改写（Paraphrase）

改写是用自己的语言清楚地重述另一个人的观点或想法。改写并不改变原文表达的意思，只是通过改变词语或者句子结构等各种方法来表达原文的含义。以下是改写的常用方法，我们可以比较一下原句和改写版本之间的区别。

7.2.1 同义词、近义词词组转换

例1：The researchers' experiment produced an unexpected result.

例2：The researchers' experiment generated an unexpected outcome.

使用同义词代替原句中的一些单词，如例1中的单词"produce"改为了"generate"，"result"改为了"output"。

7.2.2 主动语态和被动语态的转换

例1：There are signs that the government may make serious efforts in the near future.

例2：There are signs that more serious efforts may be made soon.

例1中的主动语态变成了被动语态，这样可以最大限度地保留原句的意思。又如：

例1：Increases in the cost of air travel have had a negative effect on tourism in destinations such as Hawaii, which are significant distances from other countries.

例2：The tourism in destinations which are far away from other countries, such as Hawaii, has been negatively affected by the increases of air travel fee.

7.2.3 句子语序的改变

例1：Plants are sensitive to their environment.

例2：Environment plays a vital role in the growth of plants.

例2中句子的顺序已经改变，但意思不变。这种改写方法很考验作者对于原文的理解程度。又如：

例1：The fact that certain blood types are more vulnerable to particular kinds of diseases has been proven, but there has never been credible research that links blood types to certain personality traits.

例2：It has been proven that certain blood types are more vulnerable to particular diseases, but no research has been done to link blood types to certain personality traits.

7.2.4 肯定和否定句式的切换

例1：Nowadays, people try to make themselves instantly accessible to everyone at all times.

例2：Nowadays, people never allow themselves the inconvenience of being temporarily unavailable.

只要不改变原句的意思，我们可以在改写时将否定结构改为肯定结构，反之亦然。又如：

例1：Reliable sources can be found from the governmental organizations because they usually have the resources and expertise to provide official information.

例2：Governmental organizations usually wouldn't release unreliable sources since they have the resources and expertise to provide official information.

7.2.5 非人称结构（Impersonal Structure）

例1：More and more people are aware of the inadequacies of our judicial system.

例2：There has been an increasing awareness of the inadequacies of our judicial system.

上例中例1的主语是"people"，例2在改写后使用了非人称结构，保留原句的意思，改写后的句子也显得很正式。又如：

例1：Many of the students confused the greenhouse effect with global warming and described it by listing the causes of global warming.

例2：Confusion about the greenhouse effect and global warming resulted in the students listing the causes of the latter to describe the former.

7.2.6 词性（Part of Speech）的改变

例1：To build your vocabulary is to study regularly.

例2：The most effective way to build your vocabulary is to study on a regular basis.

改变词性也是一种常见的改写方法。例1中的副词 regularly 被改为 on a regular basis。又如：

例1：In 2011, Africa became the largest cell phone market after Asia. With 600 million users, the size and quality of Africa's cell network is developing rapidly to meet the growing demand of users.

例2：Africa's cell network is expanding and up-grading rapidly to satisfy as many as 600 cell phone users in 2011. This also has made Africa the second largest cell phone market after Asia.

下面的例子则显示了一个错误的和一个正确的改写：

原句：Passing students who have not mastered the work cheats them and the employers who expect graduates to have basic skills.

如果把这句话改成：When we pass students who have not mastered the work, we cheat them and the employers who expect graduates to have particular skills. 这实际上是一个不正确的改写，因为它与原句过于相似。

而如果改写成：It is not fair to pass students who have not done strong work in school. She argues that passing these students will hurt them in their future careers.

这种改写几乎没有使用原话或短语。好的改写表明你已经理解了原文的意思，并且用自己的话重新解释了主要观点。

7.3 总结（Summarize）

总结指的是用相对较短的文字解释一个观点，主要是通过对原文大意的理解以及核心内容的把握去呈现自己的理解，是对原文的内容进行归纳并总结，呈现形式比较灵活。而改写是用自己的语言详细地解释一个观点，不能改变原文的意义，主要从原文中提炼信息。在学术写作中，对文献的总结可以帮助作者或是研究者更好地理解文本，特别是确定文献中的研究观点，并在文献综述中引用其研究的观点来支持自己的观点。

以下是总结观点时要注意的三个方面：

- 重点（focus）：只在总结中包括文献的主要观点和最重要的观点；
- 改写（paraphrase）：避免与原文重复；
- 语言风格（language style）：保持与原文相同的语言风格。

总结观点时可以按照以下步骤进行：

- 先阅读原始文献，准确理解原文主旨；
- 用自己的语言改写原文；
- 把改写的内容和原文进行对比；
- 如果有和原文意义不一样的地方再进行修改。

阅读以下段落并进行段落总结练习，再将你写的总结与给出的总结范例进行比较。

① When one hears the term "reality" applied to a television show, one might expect that the events occurred naturally or, at the least, were not scripted, but this is not always the case. Many reality shows occur in unreal environments, like rented mansions occupied by film crews. These living environments do not reflect what most people understand to be "reality." Worse, there have been accusations that events not captured on film were later restaged by producers. Worse still, some involved in the production of "reality" television claim that the participants were urged to act out story lines premeditated by producers. With such accusations floating around, it's no wonder many people take reality TV to be about as real as the sitcom.

② There are many types of lethal venom in the animal kingdom, but perhaps no stranger carrier than the platypus. The platypus is one of few venomous mammals. Males carry a venom cocktail in their ankle spurs that paralyzes victims with excruciating pain. Stranger still, the platypus is the only mammal that uses electroreception. What this means is that the platypus uses its bill to sense the electricity produced by the muscular movements of its prey. The platypus neither sees, hears, nor smells its prey while hunting but, rather, pursues it through electroreception. Perhaps most odd, the platypus is the only mammal that lays eggs rather than giving birth to live young. The platypus is an odd creature indeed.

③ Yellowstone National Park is mainly located in Wyoming, although three percent is located in the state of Montana. The Continental Divide of North America runs diagonally through the southwestern part of the park. The park sits on the Yellowstone Plateau, which is an average elevation of 8,000 feet above sea level. This plateau is bounded on nearly all sides by mountain ranges. There are 290 waterfalls that are at least fifteen feet in the park, the highest being the Lower Falls of the Yellowstone River, which falls 308 feet.

总结范例：

① Reality TV shows are not very realistic because they are filmed in unrealistic places, may contain restaged events, and may be scripted.

② The platypus is a strange mammal because it has venom, uses its beak to sense prey, and lays eggs.

③ Yellowstone Park, in Wyoming, is on a large plateau and has a bunch of waterfalls.

对于英语不是母语的作者来说，要改写英语句子或是用自己的话总结不是件容易的事情，这也是为什么作者经常面临查重率过高的原因之一。但无论是改写还是总结，都须确保没有改变原文的意义，降低与原文的相似度，同时保持自己的语言风格。最重要的是，不要忘记加文献标注。

写作实践 Writing Tasks

▶▶ **Paraphrase the following sentences. The paraphrased sentences should be grammatically different from the original ones while maintaining the same ideas.**

(1) There has never been any credible research that links blood types to certain personality traits.

(2) The fact that science is developing very quickly around the globe has made the problem far worse.

(3) Most people agree that the government must regulate the money supply.

(4) Motivation had been the subject of numerous studies for educational purposes.

(5) By analyzing the above literature, it can be seen that carbon emissions contribute greatly to global warming.

(6) Employees can be less productive at home because of distractions such as television.

(7) Findings in the study were consistent with the view that this is a result of objective conditions.

(8) Genetic engineering may offer many benefits especially for the developing countries.

(9) There is no solution to this problem except the international control of atomic energy.

10) The fact that global warming causes the change of weather often escapes many people's notice.

▶▶ Read the following passage. Write a paragraph of about 120~140 words to summarize the main ideas.

The Effectiveness of the Garbage Classification Regulation in Shanghai[1]

Discussion

The purpose of this study was to evaluate the effectiveness of the newly-released PDGCA, and to analyze the factors that hinder the regulation from effective execution. The results show that the citizens' habits of garbage classification were not formed and the situation of implementing the regulation was not satisfactory. There are several explanations for its failure. First, most respondents lacked the knowledge of garbage management procedures though they had positive attitudes toward garbage classification. They attributed the lack of the knowledge to the poor publicity of garbage classification as 70% failed to give a definite answer. Second, work pressure and family pressure affected the formation of the habit. The interview shows that the elderly were more willing to adapt to the regulation and more actively engaged in garbage classification as they had more leisure time. Third, the incentive and supervision systems are not efficient.

The effective practice of garbage classification depends on sanitation workers as well as residents. For example, sanitation workers increased workload was not subsidized correspondingly. The study also suggests that a considerable number of sanitation workers were not qualified enough for effective garbage classification, and thus professional training is urgently needed.

The findings of this study are partially consistent with some of the previous studies(Fukuyama, 2000), where publicity, residents level of education and the incentive system are major contributing

---

1 来自《谷歌学术》官方网站。

factors. The data and interview of this study show that the cultivation of the residents' habit and knowledge of garbage management process play a more important part. No significant correlation, however, is found between the level of education and participation in garbage classification. The incentive system does not seem to function in Shanghai as well.It is surmised that the incentive might be so small that it could not attract most residents.

Overall, there are several suggestions to improve the effectiveness of regulation on garbageclassification.First,the habit of garbage classification should be cultivated from an early age. In Japan where garbage classification has been successfully executed for decades, the awareness of garbage classification is instilled into kindergarten children and the program of environment protection is incorporated into primary education (Dou et al. 2012). Second, the garbage management procedure should be publicized and the instructions for garbage classification should be simple and concise. Confusion might be avoided primarily at the stage of cultivating residents' habit of garbage classification. Finally,the government should establish professional garbage classification companies. Australia has professional garbage management companies are set up and supervised by the government who can effectively help train qualified garbage management workers (Peng, 2011). Government intervention is needed in China where a sustainable profit chain has not yet formed in the garbage management industry.

The respondents are mainly young adults, while the interviewees are composed of seniors. Thus, the sample of this study, although balanced overall, has certain limitations. Hence the results of the study should be treated with caution. Further research is recommended to analyze, on alarger and more balanced scale, the factors that influence domestic garbage classification.

第 8 单元　模糊限制语
Unit 8　Hedging Language

学习目标 Learning Objectives

1. 了解学术英语写作的严谨性和逻辑性；
2. 掌握模糊限制语的写作方法和规律。

课前任务 Pretask

比较下列几组句子，判断每组中哪几句话的表达更为严谨。

Group 1:

- Education may reduce crime.
- It appears that education reduces crime.
- Education reduces crime.

Group 2

- This is possibly caused by the effects of global warming.
- This may be caused by the effects of global warming.
- This is caused by the effects of global warming.

Group 3:

- Chinese students often make mistakes with tenses.
- Chinese students always make mistakes with tenses.

引言 Introduction

模糊限制语（hedging language）是英语学术论文中必不可少的写作策略，它能表明作者的科学态度和对同行的尊重，也能够体现写作的严谨性、逻辑性、思辨性。

知识要点 Key Knowledge

字典对于 hedge 的相关解释为：to avoid giving a direct answer to a question or promising to support a particular idea, etc. 因此不难理解，hedging 就是避免直接回答问题。在学术英语写作中，我们可以把它理解为：尽量不要使用比较"绝对"的语言，将语言软化，把话说得更有余地。越是绝对的表达，越容易露出"破绽"。

在学术研究领域，严谨性是最基本的条件。无论是自然科学所需的实验数据还是人文社科所用的文献，精确地理解、阐述、论证是一切研究的基础。那么，怎样培养研究者的严谨性呢？一个很重要的步骤就是从提高语言的精确性开始。但是这里所谓的"精确性"并不是语法正确和拼写正确等基本要求，而是指概念表达的精准度，最典型的就是英文中的模糊限制语。使用模糊限制语可以使论文中的论述更客观，语气更婉转，更容易让人接受。

阅读下面的三句话，体会哪句话的表达更为严谨：

例 1：Academic dishonesty has been plaguing colleges and universities for generation.

例 2：It seems that academic dishonesty has plagued colleges and universities for generations.

例 3：Academic dishonesty might have plagued colleges and universities for generations.

又如：

例 1：Unemployment causes crime.

例 2：Unemployment tends to cause crime.

例 3：Unemployment may cause crime.

上面这两组句子乍看之下似乎没有太大的区别，但其实它们在表达层面的精准度存在着显著的差异。英语口语也常使用模糊限制语，大多是为了表示谦和礼貌。但在学术写作中，模糊限制语的使用足以体现作者作为研究者的表达甚至是思维是否足够严谨，也就是精确性（preciseness）。对比下面一组句子，一个使用了模糊限制语，一个用了比较绝对的陈述语句：

例 1：The fire was probably caused by a fault in the engine temperature gauge.

例 2：The fire could have been caused by a fault in the engine temperature gauge.

虽然上面这两句话中都使用了模糊限制语 probably 和 could，但它们也有区别。probably 的肯定性更强烈，说明有非常大的可能性；而 could 相对来说肯定性较弱，说明有一定的可能性，但是可能性不如例 1 那么大。

在学术讨论中，"万事无绝对"。我们在展开论点时要非常注意过于"绝对"的词汇，如 can、will、absolute、for sure，等等。也就是说，在陈述观点时，首先要确保所表达的意思是准确的，不能太武断，表达要留有余地（掌握多种模糊限制语的使用）。研究者可以通过阅读学术文章、参加学术讲座，以及专项的语法和词汇学习掌握精确表达的方法，并且在口语表达和写作过程中运用这些精确的表达方法。

以下是常见的模糊限制语用法：

- 通过系动词（introductory verbs）弱化因果关系：seem、tend、look like、appear to be、think、believe、doubt、be sure、indicate、suggest；
- 使用动词（lexical verbs）：believe、assume、suggest；
- 使用情态动词（modal verbs）：will、must、would、may、might、could；
- 加限定条件的副词（adverbs of frequency）：often、sometimes、usually；
- 使用情态副词（modal adverbs）：certainly、definitely、clearly、probably、possibly、perhaps、conceivably；
- 使用情态形容词（modal adjectives）：certain、definite、clear、probable、possible；
- 使用情态名词（modal nouns）：assumption、possibility、probability。

有些模糊限制语按照学科划分，使用频率也有所不同，如 may 和 can。may 在社会科学中的使用率要明显高与自然科学，而 can 却恰恰相反，这主要因为社会科学侧重逻辑推理，而自然科学则要用实验数据来说话。有趣的是，无论是社会科学还是自然科学，都较少使用 might，这是由于 might 在表达可能性时的语气最弱，容易被认为对研究命题缺乏信心，使作者处于不利地位。尽管模糊限制语能够使行文减少争议，显得礼貌。但应该注意的是，这种写作策略也是有其弊端的，过多地使用模糊限制语会使文章语气显得不可靠且啰唆。模糊限制语的使用不只是语言学习，也是提高学术严谨性的基本方法之一，是提高学术素养的重要一步。只有通过利用语言不断地修正自己的思维习惯和模式，才能真正地培养严谨治学的学术精神。

写作实践 Writing Tasks

▶▶ Read the sentences. Rewrite them using hedging language we have learned from this unit. More than one option may be possible.

(1) People aged under 25 use the Internet more frequently than older people.

Example: Typically, people aged under 25 tend to use the internet more frequently than older people.

_____

_____

(2) Despite a number of minor problems, the scheme was very successful.
_____
_____

(3) Coral reefs are seriously affected by rises in sea temperature.
_____
_____

(4) Solar power offers a solution to producing clean, cheap energy in developing countries.
_____
_____

(5) The study shows that bilingual children have better memory skills than children who only speak one language.
_____
_____

▶▶ **Spot the hedging language in the following sentences.**

(1) It is often thought that many young people tend to eat food which may be considered to be unhealthy. Although some youngsters might go to fast food outlets quite regularly when compared to older age groups, evidence suggests that in general this assumption is largely untrue.

(2) Sometimes building in rural areas can deliver a better outcome for certain communities.

(3) Data suggests that homes built in the countryside are often in a higher price bracket and thus, unattainable to most home buyers.

(4) The impact of the UK's ageing population will arguably lead to increased welfare costs. Consequently, this will probably result in higher taxes and an increased retirement age for many younger people.

(5) It could be suggested that the main concerns for the future generations are probably going to be global food supplies and population growth. This seems to suggest that both of these should be addressed by international leaders within the next five years.

第三部分　五段式短文

Part 3　Five-paragraph Essay Writing

内容提要
Preview

第三部分介绍五段式短文的写作方法。五段式短文不仅是一种写作模式，也是一种写作风格和写作思维，是学习者应该掌握的一种经典写作结构。本部分包括四个单元，第 9 单元概述五段式短文结构，初步介绍其写作框架；第 10、11、12 单元按照英语短文的写作过程展开介绍五段式短文的写作步骤。第 10 单元讲述写作前的思考过程，包括如何理解写作主题、确定观点和起草大纲；第 11 单元详细介绍五段式短文开头段、主体段和结尾段的写作方法；第 12 单元按照五段式短文的写作要点介绍如何修改短文。这部分的讲解使学习者对英语短文的基本结构有所掌握，为今后学习和工作中的各类英语写作任务打下扎实的基础。

他人就某一研究问题或某一研究领域的观点和结论，既是对他人研究成果的尊重，也有助于增强本研究的说服力。引用（citation）的格式要使用参考文献的学术格式，稍有不妥，或许会被视为剽窃（plagiarism）。参考文献中每一条文献的详细信息（如作者姓名、年份、标题、刊物名、卷期和页码等）的格式不能随意，须参照指定的规范格式。

参考文献常见格式：

- MLA style（Modern Language Association）现代言语协会格式
- APA style（American Psychological Association）美国心理学会格式
- CMS（Chicago Manual of Style）芝加哥格式
- AMA style（American Medical Association）美国医学协会格式
- 中华人民共和国国标文后参考文献著录规则 GB/T 7714—2015

写作实践 Writing Tasks

▶▶ Read the following sentences. Match them to the functions marked A, B, C, D and E.

A. Establishing the specific topic and providing the relevant background information.

B. Stating the purpose of the present study.

C. Describing the previous studies on the topic.

D. Stating the results of the present study.

E. Introducing the present methodology.

(1) The term "genetically modified organisms" (GMOs) refers to plants, microbes and animals with genes transferred from other species in order to produce certain novel characteristics.

Function: _____

(2) Wistar rats were used as the subjects in the experiment.

Function: _____

(3) The objective of this study was to assess the characteristics of fraud in medical research.

Function: _____

(4) Breast feeding, a traditional infant-feeding practice in Nigeria, has undergone a serious decline recently.

Function: _____

第 9 单元　五段式短文简介
Unit 9　An Introduction to Five-paragraph Essay

学习目标 Learning Objectives

1. 了解五段式短文结构；
2. 了解五段式短文写作步骤。

课前任务 Pretask

1. 好的英语短文的标准是什么？试找一篇文章举例说明。

2. 你是否对英语写作感兴趣？在遇到一个令你感到困惑的写作任务时，你有什么好方法帮你完成它？

引言 Introduction

　　短文是围绕一个观点、由几个段落组成的一篇文章。在一篇短文中，作者可以用多种写作模式全面地论证一个观点。短文的中心思想或观点被称为观点句（thesis statement or thesis sentence）。观点句出现在引言段，扩展段落展开论述观点句，结尾段落结束整篇文章。

　　短文写作帮助学习者理解和深入思考一个主题，也可以训练学习者的思维习惯和写作模式。学习者在一开始对写作任务感到不知所措时，可以先了解写作过程并将其分解为若干写作步骤。五段式短文是英语写作的基本结构，对学习者的语篇能力和英语思维能力的培养尤为重要。本单元主要介绍五段式短文的结构和写作步骤。

知识要点 Key Knowledge

9.1 五段式短文结构 (The Structure of Five-paragraph Essay)

范例[1]：

Noise Pollution

Natural sounds-waves, wind, birdsong-are so soothing that companies sell recordings of them to anxious people seeking a relaxing atmosphere at home or in the car. One reason why "environmental sounds" are big business is that ordinary citizens, especially city dwellers, are bombarded by noise pollution. On the way to work, on the job, and on the way home, the typical urban resident must cope with a continuing barrage of unpleasant sounds.

A trip to work at 6 or 7 am isn't quiet. No matter which route a worker takes, there is bound to be a noisy construction site somewhere along the way. Hard hats will shout from third-story windows to warn their coworkers below before heaving debris out and sending it crashing to earth. Meanwhile huge frontend loaders will crunch into these piles of rubble and back up, their warning signals letting out loud, jarring beeps. Then air hammers begin an earsplitting chorus of rat-a-tat-tat sounds guaranteed to shatter sanity as well as concrete. Before reaching the office, the worker is already completely frazzled.

The noise level in an office can be unbearable. From 9 a.m. to 5 p.m., phones and fax machines ring, computer keyboards chatter, intercoms buzz, and copy machines thump back and forth. Every time the receptionists can't find people, they resort to a nerve-shattering public address system. And because the managers worry about the employees' morale, they graciously provide the endless droning of canned music. This effectively eliminates any possibility of a moment of blessed silence.

Even traveling home from work provides no relief from the noisiness of the office. The ordinary sounds of blaring taxi horns and rumbling buses are occasionally punctuated by the ear-piercing screech of car brakes. Taking a shortcut through the park will bring the weary worker face to face with chanting religious cults, freelance musicians, screaming children, and barking dogs. But none of these sounds can compare with the large radios many park visitors

---

[1] 兰甘. 2014. 美国大学英语写作（第九版）. 北京：外语教学与研究出版社.

carry. Each radio blasts out something different, from heavy-metal rock to baseball, at decibel levels so strong that they make eardrums throb in pain. If there are birds singing or wind in the trees, the harried commuter will never hear them.

　　Noise pollution is as dangerous as any other kind of pollution. The endless pressure of noise probably triggers countless nervous breakdowns, vicious arguments, and bouts of depression. And imagine the world problems we could solve, if only the noise stopped long enough to let us think.

　　这篇文章"Noise pollution"是一篇标准的五段式短文：由一段引言、三段正文和一段结语组成，字数超过 350 字。下面将说明这些段落的功能。

9.1.1　引言段（Introductory Paragraph）

　　引言段通常以几个能吸引读者兴趣的句子开始，然后提出全文的观点句。引言段还可以包括一个短文的发展计划（plan of development）："预览"支持观点句的支撑点。这些支撑点应该按照它们在正文中出现的顺序排列。上篇文章"Noise Pollution"引言段的观点句为"On the way to work, on the job, and on the way home, the typical urban resident must cope with a continuing barrage of unpleasant sounds."，而正文部分则是按照"On the way to work, on the job, and on the way home"这一发展计划的顺序展开论述。

9.1.2　正文段（Body Paragraph）

　　五段式短文有三个支点，分别在三个独立的正文段落中展开，当然，更为复杂的文章需要四个或更多的正文段落来支持观点。每一个正文段落都应以一个主题句开始，阐述该段中要详细阐述的观点。正如观点句是整篇文章的核心，主题句是每一个正文段的中心。

9.1.3　结语段（Concluding Paragraph）

结论段通常简要重申观点句，总结主要支撑点，还可提出结论性的思考。

以下是五段式短文的基本结构：

Titile of the Essay

▶▶ **Introduction**

Opening remarks to catch reader's interest

Thesis statement

Essay signpost (optional)

▶▶ **Body**

Topic sentence 1 (supporting point 1)

    Specific evidence

Topic sentence 2 (supporting point 2)

    Specific evidence

Topic sentence 3 (supporting point 3)

    Specific evidence

▶▶ **Conclusion**

Summary

General closing remarks

9.2 五段式短文的好处（Benefits of Writing Five-paragraph Essays）

第一，五段式短文的基本结构观点突出，结构清晰，逻辑严密，适用于包括叙述、描述、例证、过程、原因和/或效果、比较和/或对比、定义、分类和论证等类型的短文（narration, description, exemplification, process, cause and/or effect, comparison and/or contrast, definition, division-classification, and argument）。这种结构对论文和研究报告也适用。

第二，学习五段式短文的写作方法可以提高学习者的阅读和演讲技能。作为一名读者，你会更加批判地意识到其他作者的观点和（或未能提供）支持这些观点的证据。五段式短文的写作技能将会使你更自信地应付三个基本部分：吸引人的引言部分、坚实的主体部分和全面的结论。

第三，五段式短文写作技能能够培养学习者的思考能力。完成一篇五段式短文要求学习者仔细整理、思考和组织观点和论述依据，学会表达想法，并合乎逻辑地进行论述和总结，这一写作过程将有效地训练思维能力。

9.3 写作步骤概述（Overview of the Writing Process）

后文将把五段式短文的写作方法分解成一系列步骤：从理解题目、选择素材，到确定观点句、拟定大纲，再到完成初稿、修改结构和内容，等等。

▶▶ **Getting Started**

Understanding the assignment

Part 3　Five-paragraph Essay Writing

Selecting a subject

Collecting information

▶▶ **Planning**

Forming a thesis

Developing a plan or an outline

▶▶ **Drafting**

Opening your draft

Developing the middle

Ending your draft

▶▶ **Revising**

Improving ideas, organization, and voice

Editing for style

Proofreading for correctness

写作实践 Writing Tasks

▶▶ Read "Noise Pollution" on Page 80 again. Answer the following questions.

(1) In the first paragraph, which sentence presents the thesis of the essay?

(2) How does the writer present his/her plan or development of this essay in the thesis?

(3) What is the topic sentence for the second, third and fourth paragraph?

(4) What kind of details does the writer use in each body paragraph to support the topic sentence? Try to make a list of supporting details for each body paragraph.

(5) How does the writer conclude the essay? What is the function of each sentence in the concluding paragraph?

第 10 单元　谋篇布局
Unit 10　Planning an Essay

学习目标 Learning Objectives

1. 学习如何判断主题；
2. 学习如何确定个人观点；
3. 学习如何组织论点和论据。

课前任务 Pretask

请选择一个话题进行课前线上或线下小组讨论，每位小组成员的发言内容包括对话题的理解、思考过程、观点及写作要点等，由一位小组成员进行总结并在课堂上汇报。

引言 Introduction

当你计划写一篇文章时，需要了解写作话题和写作目的，同时需要搜集一些相关信息和他人的观点，并思考两个问题：（1）如何确立写作主题和观点；（2）如何组织用于支撑观点的细节内容。在开始写文章之前，准备一个简单的大纲会很有用，包括观点、写作要点和基本细节。本单元主要讲述写作前的准备、观点句的写作方法以及如何拟定大纲。

知识要点 Key Knowledge

10.1　写作前的准备（Getting Started）

10.1.1　理解主题和写作目的（Understanding the Subject and the Writing Purpose）

思想内容是写作的实质，如果没有丰富的思想，就不能满足读者的需要，也就不能达到写作的目的。理解主题包括收集相关的细节，如背景、现状、影响等，这些细节将决定文

章内容和组织结构。写作题目中的关键词表明了写作目的,请看下面这些常见的关键词及其可表达的写作目的:

> Analyze: 将一个主题分解成子部分,显示这些部分是如何关联的;
> Argue: 用逻辑论证来捍卫一项主张;
> Classify: 将一个大的组划分为子组;
> Compare/contrast: 指出相同点和不同点;
> Define: 对某事给出一个清晰的定义或意义;
> Describe: 详细展示某物是什么样的;
> Evaluate: 衡量事物的真实性或有用性;
> Explain: 给出原因,列出步骤,讨论原因;
> Interpret: 用自己的话解释某事的意思;
> Reflect: 分享对一个主题深思熟虑的想法;
> Summarize: 用自己的话简短地复述别人的观点。

10.1.2 缩小主题范围(Limit the Subject Area)

选择一个和主题相关的、更具体的话题,这样有利于在文章中展开深入论述。正如以下两个例子所示,概括的主题和具体的主题是有区别的:

例1: General Subject Area: College life
　　　Limited Topic: Sports activities

例2: General Subject Area: Chinese education
　　　Limited Topic: Chinese child-raising

10.1.3 想法的产生(Brainstorming)

写作前需要一个思考过程,帮助学习者厘清写作思路,选择写作要点,从一个和主题相关的概念开始,自由地列出想法(也称为"头脑风暴")。下例是关于 Life threatening stress 这一主题的想法清单:

> Life threatening stress:
> - Unconscious
> - Threat
> - Health

- Self-defense system
- Decrease in body's natural immune function
- Potential danger
- Heart disease
- Blood pressure
- Risk of developing cancer
- Risk of stroke

10.2 观点句的写作（Forming Thesis Statement）

10.2.1 观点句的功能（Function of Thesis Statement）

文章是围绕作者想要表达的中心观点展开的，通常在引言部分提出包含有中心观点的句子，即观点句。观点句首先告诉读者一篇文章的主题；其次表达了作者的态度，观点或想法，还可以包含主要论述内容。以下是观点句写作的要点。

10.2.2 确定具体的主题（Find a Focus）

写作前的思考可以使学习者对主题有更深的了解，进而选择一个特别的主题（specific topic）。下例展示了如何将主题从宽泛到具体：

General subject: Psychological Health

Limited topic: Stress and Depression

Specific topic: Teenagers and Stress

10.2.3 观点句的三个要素 (Three Parts of Thesis Statement）

写作的第一步是确定观点句，即用一个句子来表达作者对主题的态度或想法，可参考下面的写作公式：

一个具体的主题 + 一个具体的观点 + 主要论述内容（可选择）= 一个观点句

例1：a specific focus (Internet) + a specific claim (causes addictions) + essay signpost (three types of Internet addictions: online relationships addiction, net gaming and irresistible web surfing) = an effective thesis statement

例1的观点句为：

The three main types of Internet addictions caused by Internet are online relationships addiction, net gaming and irresistible web surfing.

10.2.4 观点句常见错误（Common Mistakes in Writing Thesis Statement）

观点句写作常见的错误包括：（1）用疑问句提出观点；（2）宣布主题而不是陈述主题；（3）主题太宽泛；（4）观点句包含多个论点。

1. 用疑问句提出观点（Write questions, not answers）

例1: What should be done to encourage people to protect environment?

例2: Are the problems that international travelers cause greater than the advantages they bring?

上例中的两个句子虽然提出了问题，但并没有明确表达作者的观点。修改后的观点句如下：

例1: Government should take the initiative to encourage individuals to protect the earth.

例2: I believe the advantages international travelers bring to the countries they choose to visit outweigh the negatives.

2. 宣布主题而不是陈述主题（Write Statements, not announcements）

例1: The subject of this paper will be the main purpose of school.

例2: The movement of people from agricultural areas to cities is the concern of this essay.

上例中的两个句子不是观点句，而是主题声明，没有表达作者观点的关键词。修改后的观点句如下：

例1: School should aim to cultivate students' personal interests, train their comprehensive skills and supply them moral standards.

例2: The movement of people from agricultural areas to cities causes serious problems such as overpopulation in urban areas, high rate of unemployment and the increasing number of left-behind children in rural areas.

3. 主题太宽泛（Statements that are too broad）

例1: People's way of life has changed a lot.

例2: Most of people in the world could get access to Internet.

上例中的两个句子主题都过于宽泛，无法在短文中得到充分的论述。主题应该足够具体，修改后的观点句如下：

例1: Technology has changed people's way of life in many areas, such as the world of business, entertainment, and education.

例2: We can not totally believe the information on Internet because they might be imprecise, and untrustworthy.

4. 观点句包含多个观点（Statements develop more than one idea）

例1: One of the purposes of learning a second language is to communicate with native speakers, and it is important to know the culture and tradition in foreign countries.

例2: Zoos play very important role in providing entertainment for people, and it also help scientists to do researchers on wild animals.

上例中的两个句子都包含不止一个观点，一篇文章只能表达一个主要观点。修改后的观点句如下：

例1: One of the purposes of learning a second language is to communicate with native speakers.

例2: Zoos play very important role in providing entertainment for people.

10.3 拟定大纲（Developing a Plan or an Outline）

在确定观点句以后，应该拟定文章大纲。仔细考虑观点，有序地论述观点的依据。大纲是文章的计划或蓝图，对于完成一篇五段式短文尤为重要。大纲需要列出每个段落的核心内容以及基本细节，常见的大纲类型有两种：

10.3.1 主题提纲（Topic Outline）

主题大纲一般用短语呈现文章要点和基本细节，如：

Noise Pollution

Thesis: On the way to work, on the job, and on the way home, the typical urban resident must cope with a continuing barrage of unpleasant sounds.

Introductory paragraph:

    Natural sounds

    City dwellers, noise pollution

Body paragraph I

A trip to work

Noisy construction

Body paragraph II

The noise level in an office

From nine to five o'clock

Body paragraph III

Traveling home from work

The ordinary sounds of blaring taxi horns and rumbling buses

The large radios many park visitors carry

Concluding paragraph

The endless pressure of noise

Vicious arguments, bouts of depression

10.3.2 句子大纲（Sentence Outline）

句子大纲一般用完整句呈现文章要点和细节，如在以上主题大纲的基础上进一步发展而成的句子大纲。

Noise Pollution

Thesis: On the way to work, on the job, and on the way home, the typical urban resident must cope with a continuing barrage of unpleasant sounds.

Introductory paragraph:

Natural sounds are so soothing that companies sell recordings of them to anxious people seeking a relaxing atmosphere at home or in the car. One reason why "environmental sounds" are big business is that ordinary citizens, especially city dwellers, are bombarded by noise pollution.

Body paragraph I

Main idea: A trip to work at 6 or 7 am isn't quiet.

Supporting details:

1. There is bound to be a noisy construction site somewhere along the way.

2. Hard hats will shout from third-story windows to warn their coworkers below before heaving debris out and sending it crashing to earth.

3. Huge frontend loaders will crunch into these piles of rubble and back up, their warning signals letting out loud, jarring beeps.

4. Air hammers begin an earsplitting chorus of rat-a-tat-tat sounds guaranteed to shatter sanity as well as concrete.

Body paragraph II

Main idea: The noise level in an office can be unbearable.

Supporting details:

1. From 9 am to 5 pm, phones and fax machines ring, computer keyboards chatter, intercoms buzz, and copy machines thump back and forth.

2. Every time the receptionists can't find people, they resort to a nerve-shattering public address system.

3. And because the managers worry about the employees' morale, they graciously provide the endless droning of canned music.

Body paragraph III

Main idea: Traveling home from work provides no relief from the noisiness of the office.

Supporting details:

1. The ordinary sounds of blaring taxi horns and rumbling buses are occasionally punctuated by the ear-piercing screech of car brakes.

2. The large radios many park visitors carry. Each radio blasts out something different, from heavy-metal rock to baseball, at decibel levels so strong that they make eardrums throb in pain.

Concluding paragraph

Noise pollution is as dangerous as any other kind of pollution. And imagine the world problems we could solve, if only the noise stopped long enough to let us think.

写作实践 Writing Tasks

▶▶ Read the following general subject areas. Generate a limited topic for each of them.

(1) General Subject Area: interpersonal relationships

Limited Topic:

(2) General Subject Area: Children and school education

   Limited Topic: _____

(3) General Subject Area: The effect of social media

   Limited Topic: _____

(4) General Subject Area: Business

   Limited Topic: _____

(5) General Subject Area: Life in university

   Limited Topic: _____

▶▶ **Complete the following thesis statements by writing the signpost according to the given specific focus and specific claim.**

(1) A specific focus: The main function of a university

   A specific claim: Universities should provide graduates with some important qualities.

   Essay signpost: _____

(2) A specific focus: The increasing use of social media platforms

   A specific claim: With the increasing use of social media platforms, people are losing the ability to communicate face to face.

   Essay signpost: _____

(3) A specific focus: Advertisement and consumption

   A specific claim: Advertisement affect people's options of consumption.

   Essay signpost: _____

(4) A specific focus: Enterprises and social responsibilities

   A specific claim: Enterprises should undertake social responsibilities.

   Essay signpost: _____

(5) A specific focus: Students' psychological problems

   A specific claim: Many families suffer from students' psychological problems.

   Essay signpost: _____

第 11 单元　完成初稿
Unit 11　Drafting

学习目标 Learning Objectives

1. 学习短文开头段写作步骤；
2. 学习正文段落结构和段落发展方法；
3. 学习结尾段写作步骤。

课前任务 Pretask

请找一些不同类型的英语短文，如游记、书评、社论等，并总结开头段、正文和结尾段使用的写作方法。

引言 Introduction

一篇短文的开头段是最重要的部分之一。开头段的主要作用是：(1)吸引读者；(2)确定写作方向；(3)介绍写作思路。开头段像一个漏斗，它吸引读者过渡到作者观点。观点一般放在开头段的最后一句话。短文的中间部分用于发展和支撑论点，提供详细的论据。缺乏细节描述的写作就像一幅模糊的图像，飘忽不定的内容会使文章脱离主旨。结尾段用于回顾整篇文章并澄清重点，提供值得思考的内容。本单元介绍如何完成一篇短文的初稿。

知识要点 Key Knowledge

11.1 引言段（Introductory Paragraph）

读者首先会读文章的开头部分，然后再决定是否继续阅读，因此，文章的开头部分是很重要的，既要吸引人，又要提供一些重要信息。文章的开头部分可称为引言段，引言段有三个功能：

（1）吸引读者的兴趣；

（2）提出观点句（thesis statement）：（见下文范例中的最后一句话，其中包括表明作者态度的关键信息"is harmful to adolescents"。

（3）提出文章发展方向（essay signpost），如下文范例中的"because it reduces their involvement with school, encourages a materialistic and expensive lifestyle, and increases the chance of having problems with drugs and alcohol"。但在某些情况下，essay signpost 也可以省略。

范例[1]：

> - The pressure for teenagers to work is great, and not just because of the economic plight in the world today. Much of it is peer pressure to have a little bit of freedom and independence, and to have their own spending money. The concern we have is when the part-time work becomes the primary focus. These are the words of Roxanne Bradshaw, educator and officer of the National Education Association. Many people argue that working can be a valuable experience for the young. However, working more than about fifteen hours a week is harmful to adolescents because it reduces their involvement with school, encourages a materialistic and expensive lifestyle, and increases the chance of having problems with drugs and alcohol.

11.1.1 如何使读者产生兴趣（How to Grab Readers' Interest）

1. 提供背景信息（Offer background information）

范例[2]：

> - Most children, no matter what their personal or family situation, lead more or less controlled lives. As they grow, they begin to sense the pressure of controlling factors in their lives, and start struggling to take control themselves. This can be a difficult process. In the works *Native Son* and *Equus*, Richard Wright and Peter Shaffer, respectively, create two characters who must deal with this struggle. Bigger in *Native Son* and Alan in *Equus* are both entering adulthood and have come to realize that they are controlled by work, religion, and the media. In the midst of these characters' efforts to gain control, each character falls into a tragic situation.

---

1 兰甘. 2014. 美国大学英语写作（第九版）. 北京：外语教学与研究出版社.

2 Randall V., Verne M., John V. R. & Pat S. 2009. *The College Writer: A Guide to Thinking, Writing, and Researching* (Third Edition). Boston: Wadsworth Cengage Learning, 201.

第三部分 五段式短文
Part 3 Five-paragraph Essay Writing

范例[1]：

- Known as "America's Last Frontier", the Arctic National Wildlife Refuge (ANWR) is located in the northeast corner of Alaska, right along the Beaufort Sea. President Dwight D. Eisenhower established the refuge in 1960, and today its 19 million acres make it one of the biggest refuges in the United States and home to a wide variety of wildlife such as eagles, wolves, moose, grizzly bears, polar bears, and caribou. During the last few years, however, the security of that home has been threatened by those who want to use one section of the ANWR to drill for oil. That section—named Area1002—encompasses 1.5 million acres of pristine land near the coast.

2. 数据（Statistics）

真实和可靠的数据使引言更具吸引力和说服力。

范例[2]：

- The most vulnerable victims of poverty are the world's children. Nearly 28,000 children die every day—more than 10 million per year—most from preventable diseases and malnutrition. Yet, the handful of preventable diseases that kill the majority of these children can be treated and prevented at very little cost. Measles can be prevented with a vaccine costing just 26 cents. Diarrheal disease, which results from poor sanitation and unsafe drinking water, can be treated with pennies' worth of oral rehydration salts. Malaria kills nearly one mil-lion children each year, despite the fact that treatment for acute malaria costs just pennies.

3. 用一个轶事开始（Use an anecdote）

有时简短地叙述一件事会使文章的开头更生动，如下例中作者对忙碌早晨的描述：

范例[3]：

- It was 8:00 am; her husband, Lance, had left for work without filling the tank on the

---

[1] Randall V., Verne M., John V. R. & Pat S. 2009. *The College Writer: A Guide to Thinking, Writing, and Researching* (Third Edition). Boston: Wadsworth Cengage Learning, 297.

[2] Duane R., Gregory G. & Barry M. 2009. *The McGraw-Hill Guide: Writing for College, Writing for Life (Second Edition)*. New York: MacGraw-Hill, 434.

[3] Randall V., Verne M., John V. R. & Pat S. 2009. *The College Writer: A Guide to Thinking, Writing, and Researching* (Third Edition). Boston: Wadsworth Cengage Learning, 185.

Mazda, and her daughter, Gina, had gotten on the school bus without her show-and-tell bunny. "Great", thought Jan, "now I have to get gas at Demler's, stop by Gina's school, and drop Alex off at day care—all before my 9:30 class!" Quickly she grabbed the diaper bag, picked up the baby, and headed for the door. At 9:35, with her heart pounding and hands sweating, she scrambled into the classroom, found an open seat, and was hurriedly pulling out her psych notes when the prof asked, "So... precisely what does Jung mean by 'collective unconscious'-Jan?" " Uh... what was the question? " she responded. Does the scene sound familiar—too much work, too little time, and too much stress? Actually, periods of excessive stress are just part of life in college—or out of college, for that matter. Normally, stress (the response to a perceived threat) is a powerful, life-saving force, but when stress becomes excessive, it is a life-threatening condition.

4. 提出问题（Ask a question）

用一个或几个和主题相关的问题作为引言段的开始。

范例：

- What if museums, universities and government agencies could put your dead relatives on display or keep them in boxes to be cut up and otherwise studied? What if you believed that the spirits of the dead could not rest until their human remains were placed in a sacred area? The ordinary American would say there ought to be a law—and there is, for ordinary Americans. The problem for American Indians is that there are too many laws of the kind that make us the archeological property of the United States and too few of the kind that protect us from such insults.[1]

- Have you ever been in a conversation in which you suddenly felt lost-out of the loop? Perhaps you feel that way in your literature class. You may think a poem or short story means one thing, and then your instructor suddenly pulls out the "hidden meaning". Joining the conversation about literature—in class or in an essay—may indeed seem daunting, but you can do it if you know what to look for and what to talk about. There are four main perspectives, or approaches, that you can use to converse about literature.[2]

---

1 Richard B., Maureen D. G. & Francine W. 2009. *The Norton Field Guide to Writing, with Reading and Handbook* (Second Edition). New York: W.W. Norton & Company, 286.

2 Randall V., Verne M., John V. R. & Pat S. 2009. *The College Writer: A Guide to Thinking, Writing,* and Researching (Third Edition). Boston: Wadsworth Cengage Learning, 220.

5. 定义或概念（Define key terms or concepts）

有时，论述的成败取决于关键术语的定义，可以在文章开始解释重要术语或概念。

范例[1]：

> - To many people, the word "fragrance" means something that smells nice, such as perfume. We don't often stop to think that scents are chemicals. Fragrance chemicals are organic compounds that volatilize, or vaporize into the air-that's why we can smell them. They are added to products to give them a scent or to mask the odor of other ingredients. The volatile organic chemicals (VOCs) emitted by fragrance products can contribute to poor indoor air quality (IAQ) and are associated with a variety of adverse health effects.

6. 引用（Use a quotation）

引言的目的是介绍他人的观点。引用的内容可以是一本书或一篇文章中的名言，也可以是一句流行的谚语、一则广告语或者朋友和家人最常说的话语。

范例[2]：

> - "Fish and visitors", wrote Benjamin Franklin, "begin to smell after three days", Last summer, when my sister and her family came to spend their two-week vacation with us, I became convinced that Franklin was right. After only three days of my family's visit, I was thoroughly sick of my brother-in-law's lame jokes, my sister's endless complaints about her boss, and their children's constant invasions of our privacy.

11.2　正文段 (Middle Paragraphs)

正文是文章中最重要的部分，用于论述观点句。正文既需要大量细节内容，也要在逻辑、内容上与观点句保持统一，以避免论述模糊或者内容偏离文章主题。

11.2.1　主题句（Topic Sentence）

正如观点句宣布了一篇文章的主题和观点一样，主题句陈述了正文段的主题。每一个正文段只围绕观点句的一个要点展开论述，主题句通常位于正文段的开始。

---

[1] Richard B., M. D. G. & Francine W. 2009. *The Norton Field Guide to Writing, with Reading and Handbook (Second Edition).* New York: W.W. Norton & Company, 264.

[2] 兰甘. 2014. 美国大学英语写作（第九版）. 北京：外语教学与研究出版社.

11.2.2　主题句的结构（Structure of a Topic Sentence）

主题句通常由两部分组成：

（1）具体的话题（Specific topic）

（2）作者对这一具体话题的态度或观点（The writer's attitude toward or idea about the specific topic）

作者的态度和观点通常用一个或多个关键词来表达。一个正文段中的所有细节内容都应该支持主题句的观点。

范例：

- The average teen chooses to spend an average of 16.7 hours a week reading and writing online.
- Like the most complex issues, discussions about the impact of media violence on children suffer from that commonest of media problems: fudge.

注意上例两个主题句中的主题和关键词。第一句话的主题是"the average teen"，具体陈述是"they spend an average of 16.7 hours a week reading and writing online"；第二句话的主题是"discussions about the impact of media violence on children"，具体陈述是"suffer from that commonest of media problems: fudge"。

11.2.3　段落发展方法（Methods of Paragraph Development）

1. 例证法（Exemplification）

例证能增强陈述的真实性，也能帮助读者充分理解一个观点。生动、具体的例子也能增加段落的趣味性。

范例[1]：

- Text-centered approaches focus on the literary piece itself. Often called formalist criticism, such approaches claim that the structure of a work and the rules of its genre are crucial to its meaning. The formalist critic determines how various elements (plot, character, language, and so on) reinforce the meaning and unify the work. For example, the formalist may ask the following questions concerning Robert Browning's poem *My Last Duchess*: How do the main elements in the poem-irony, symbolism, and verse form—help develop

---

[1] Randall V., Verne M., John V. R. & Pat S. 2009. *The College Writer: A Guide to Thinking, Writing, and Researching* (Third Edition). Boston: Wadsworth Cengage Learning, 220.

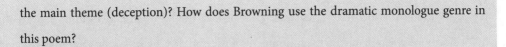

the main theme (deception)? How does Browning use the dramatic monologue genre in this poem?

2. 过程法（Process）

无论论述的过程是简单还是复杂，都需要先确定步骤，按顺序逐一解释。

范例[1]：

- Fast-food French fries are made from a baking potato like an Idaho russet, or any other variety that is mealy, or starchy, rather than waxy. The potatoes are harvested, cured, washed, peeled, sliced, and then blanched-cooked enough so that the insides have a fluffy texture but not so much that the fry gets soft and breaks. Blanching is followed by drying, and drying by a thirty-second deep fry, to give the potatoes a crisp shell. Then the fries are frozen until the moment of service, when they are deep-fried again, this time for somewhere around three minutes. Depending on the fast-food chain involved, there are other steps interspersed in this process. McDonald's fries, for example, are briefly dipped in a sugar solution, which gives them their golden-brown color; Burger King fries are dipped in a starch batter, which is what gives those fries their distinctive hard shell and audible crunch. But the result is similar. The potato that is first harvested in the field is roughly 80 percent water. The process of creating a French fry consists, essentially, of removing as much of that water as possible—through blanching, drying, and deep-frying-and replacing it with fat.

3. 因果分析法（Cause and effect）

分析有助于读者思考事情发生的原因和可能会发生什么，因果分析实际上是在论述事物的合理性或可能性，有助于更好地理解和解释事物。

范例[2]：

结果分析：

- One of the most immediate results of prolonged stress is a decrease in the body's natural

---

1　Richard B., Maureen D. G. & Francine W. 2009. *The Norton Field Guide to Writing, with Reading and Handbook* (Second Edition). New York: W.W. Norton & Company, 339.

2　Randall V., Verne M., John V. R. & Pat S. 2009. *The College Writer: A Guide to Thinking, Writing, and Researching* (Third Edition). Boston: Wadsworth Cengage Learning, 186.

> immune function. The release of cortisol into the bloodstream inhibits a protective hormone released during the immune response and thereby suppresses immune reactions. During periods of stress, the immune system becomes compromised, and the body experiences increased susceptibility to disease. For example, some studies have proven that when medical students prepare for board exams, they experience more stress and get sick more often than when they prepare for less stressful exams.

范例 [1]：

> 原因分析：
>
> - During his years as president, 1861—1865, Abraham Lincoln experienced great stress from a combination of causes. First, the Civil War, which broke out weeks after his March 1861 inauguration, wore on him daily until its end in April 1865. Second, typhoid took the life of Willie, his beloved eleven-year-old son, in February 1862. Third, his wife, Mary Todd Lincoln, suffered from depression and other forms of mental illness, problems that became more acute during the years in the White House.

4. 对比对照法（Comparison and Contrast）

比较是为了展现相似之处；对比是为了展现不同之处，比较或对比的目的是为了使读者更清楚地理解两种事物。

范例 [2]：

> - The Perfect Dog is an enticing fantasy pooch. It's the dog that instantly learns to pee outdoors, never menaces or frightens children, plays gently with other dogs, won't jump on the UPS guy, never rolls in gross things, eats only the appropriate food at the right time, and never chews anything not meant for him. This dog does not exist. The Disney Dog is the one who loves you alone, who will sacrifice his life to pull your toddler back from the busy street, who will cross 1,000 miles of towering snowdrifts to find you if you accidentally leave him behind in the Arctic.[3]

1　Duane R., Gregory G., Barry M. 2009. *The McGraw-Hill Guide: Writing for college, Writing for Life Second Edition*. New York: MacGraw-Hill, 431.

2　Cheryl G. 2008. *The Harbrace Guide to Writing*. Mason: Cengage Learning, 429.

3　Cheryl G. 2008. *The Harbrace Guide to Writing*. Mason: Cengage Learning, 408.

- Native language immersion schools are one of the best ways to breathe life into a dying language, according to Native language experts. In contrast, adult classes at tribal colleges, summer language camps, and bilingual programs in public schools rarely, if ever, produce fluent speakers. But few efforts are more difficult to start and run than an immersion school. "Every tribe wants an immersion school, but the hurdles are just tremendous," says Inee Yang Slaughter, of the Indigenous Languages Institute in New Mexico. "Most fail."

5. 定义法（Definition）

作者有时会用非正式的定义来解释一个特定术语的含义，表明作者对专业术语的个人理解。所以段落可以从一个术语开始，然后用一系列的例子来说明它的含义。

范例[1]：

- It is now estimated that more than half of the nursing-home residents in the United States have dementia. But what, exactly, is this disease? Dementia is a broad term that refers to a number of health problems, including Alzheimer's disease, brain tumors, and arteriosclerosis, the hardening of arteries to the heart. The outward symptoms of dementia are often disturbing, as this disease affects both the language skills and the behavior of the patient.

6. 分类法（Classification and Division）

分类是将事物归类，可以更好地管理或理解多种事物；划分是把一个事物分解、分割成几个部分以更好地理解和分析。

范例[2]：

- A city walker will notice that most dogs fall into one of three categories. First there are the big dogs, which are generally harmless and often downright friendly. They walk along peacefully with their masters, their tongues hanging out and big goofy grins on their faces. Apparently they know they're too big to have anything to worry about, so why not be nice? Second are the spunky medium-sized dogs. When they see a stranger approaching, they go

---

1　Randall V., Verne M., John V. R. & Pat S. 2009. *The College Writer: A guide to Thinking, Writing, and Researching* (Third Edition). Boston: Wadsworth Cengage Learning, 247.

2　兰甘 . 2019. 美国大学英语写作 . 广州：世界图书出版公司 .

> on alert. They prick up their ears, they raise their hackles, and they may growl a little deep in their throats. "I could tear you up," they seem to be saying, "but I won't if you behave yourself." Unless the walker leaps for their master's throat, these dogs usually won't do anything more than threaten. The third category is made up of the shivering neurotic little yappers whose shrill barks could shatter glass and whose needle-like little teeth are eager to sink into a friendly outstretched hand. Walkers always wonder about these dogs-don't they know that people who really wanted to could squash them under their feet like bugs? Apparently not, because of all the dogs a walker meets, these provide the most irritation. Such dogs are only one of the potential hazards that the city walker encounters.

7. 描述（Description）

描述是展现事物的样子，如声音、感觉、气味和味道等。描述性的细节是帮助读者看到（或听到、闻到等）所写的内容，因此描述法在文章中很常见。

范例[1]：

> - So what is stress? Actually, the physiological characteristics of stress are some of the body's potentially good self-defense mechanisms. Take, for example, a man who is crossing a street when he spots an oncoming car. Immediately his brain signals his adrenal glands to release a flood of adrenaline into his bloodstream. As a result, his muscles contract, his eyes dilate, his heart pounds faster, his breathing quickens, and his blood clots more readily. Each one of these responses helps the man leap out of the car's path. His muscles contract to give him exceptional strength. His eyes dilate so that he can see more clearly. His heart pumps more blood and his lungs exchange more air-both to increase his metabolism. If the man were injured, his blood would clot faster, ensuring a smaller amount of blood loss. In this situation and many more like it, stress symptoms are good.

8. 记叙（Narration）

作为一种写作方法，叙述可以用于大多数类型的文章中。叙述不只是讲有趣的故事，作者需要按照清晰的顺序叙述相关细节。

---

[1] Randall V., Verne M., John V. R. & Pat S. 2009. *The College Writer: A Guide to Thinking, Writing, and Researching* (Third Edition). Boston: Wadsworth Cengage Learning, 185.

范例[1]：

> - To Motz and similar "expert", I say this: Some of my finest childhood memories are of my best friend, Solara, coming over to my house with her pink carry-on suitcase stuffed with Barbies and their accoutrements. For hours we would play with them, giving haircuts, filling mixing bowls to make swimming pools, and creating small "campfires" so Barbie could makes' mores. Sometimes we dressed her in store-bought clothes, and sometimes we designed clothing for her. Other times we turned Barbie into the heroines in our books, and she helped us act out the plots. Playing with Barbies need not be an unimaginative, antisocial activity that promotes conformity, materialism, and superficial ideals. I played with Barbies and I'm fine. Take that, Motz!

9. 议论（Argument）

议论是指说服读者相信作者在某一问题上的立场是合理的，影响读者对某一问题的看法，或者说服读者改变观点或采取某种行动。事实上，无论写作目的是什么，所有类型的文章都是有论点的。

范例：

> - Fatherlessness is the most harmful demographic trend of this generation. It is the leading cause of declining child well-being in our society. It is also the engine driving our most urgent social problems, from crime to adolescent pregnancy to child abuse to domestic violence against women. Yet, despite its scale and social consequences, fatherlessness is a problem that is frequently ignored or denied. Especially within our elite discourse, it remains largely a problem with no name.

11.3 结束段（Concluding Paragraph）

11.3.1 结束段的写作目的（Purpose of Concluding Paragraph）

结尾段用于结束全文、总结重点，帮助读者再次理解和思考作者的观点和写作意义，留给读者值得思考的问题。作者可以尝试多种结尾方式，根据写作目的选择一个最适合的。结束段的结构通常可以分为两个部分：重申要点和激励读者。

---

[1] Randall V., Verne M., John V. R. & Pat S. 2009. *The College Writer: A Guide to Thinking, Writing, and Researching (Third Edition)*. Boston: Wadsworth Cengage Learning, 278.

1. 重申要点（Reassert the mainoint）

读者在读完一篇文章，特别是较为复杂的文章的主要内容后，需要在结尾段重新回顾文章要点。因此作者应该从论述的第一部开始，逐一总结全文要点，并且重申观点句。

2. 激励读者（Urge the reader）

对于作者来说，结束段是使读者认同、接受观点的最后机会。以下是一些常见的说服读者的写作策略，总之作者应该尽可能展现出文章的写作意义和实用价值。

① 总结和思考

范例[1]：

> - If you look at the variety of questions critics might ask about "My Last Duchess," you see both the diversity of critical approaches and the common ground between them. In fact, interpretive methods actually share important characteristics: (1) a close attention to literary elements such as character, plot, symbolism, and metaphor; (2) a desire not to distort the work; and (3) a sincere concern for increasing interest and understanding in a text. In actual practice, critics may develop a hybrid approach to criticism, one that matches their individual questions and concerns about a text. Now that you're familiar with some of the questions defining literary criticism, exercise your own curiosity (and join the ongoing literary dialogue) by discussing a text that genuinely interests you.

② 引用一段发人深省的语录

范例[2]：

> - Saving the environment is up to each of us. Levels of harmful emissions would drop dramatically if we chose to carpool or take public transportation more often. Conserving fuel and electricity at home by sealing up leaky windows and using energy-saving light bulbs would help, too. As David Orr once wrote," When we heal the Earth, we heal ourselves."

---

1 Randall V., Verne M., John V. R. & Pat S. 2009. *The College Writer: A Guide to Thinking, Writing, and Researching (Third Edition).* Boston: Wadsworth Cengage Learning, 221.

2 兰甘. 2014. 美国大学英语写作（第九版）. 北京：外语教学与研究出版社.

③ 提出有价值的问题

范例[1]：

> - No, the romance and beauty were all gone from the river. All the value any feature of it had for me now was the amount of usefulness it could furnish toward compassing the safe piloting of a steamboat. Since those days, I have pitied doctors from my heart. What does the lovely flush in a beauty's cheek mean to a doctor but a "break" that ripples above some deadly disease? Are not all her visible charms sown thick with what are to him the signs and symbols of hidden decay? Does he ever see her beauty at all, or doesn't he simply view her professionally, and comment upon her unwholesome condition all to himself? And doesn't he sometimes wonder whether he has gained most or lost most by learning his trade?

④ 提出预测或建议

范例[2]：

> - So what is the best "medication" for people with dementia? While no treatment can stop the illness, understanding the disease and its symptoms is the key to helping people cope. Doctors who understand the science of dementia can prescribe medicine. However, all of us who understand the heartbreaking symptoms and effects of the disease can provide another, possibly more effective treatment. We can respond to the victim of dementia with patience, kindness, and love.

⑤ 呼吁行动

范例[3]：

> - Agroterrorism has not yet been used on a large scale anywhere on the globe. However, its

---

1 Randall V., Verne M., John V. R. & Pat S. 2009. *The College Writer: A Guide to Thinking, Writing, and Researching (Third Edition).* Boston: Wadsworth Cengage Learning, 204.

2 Randall V., Verne M., John V. R. & Pat S. 2009. *The College Writer: A Guide to Thinking, Writing, and Researching (Third Edition).* Boston: Wadsworth Cengage Learning, 249.

3 Randall V., Verne M., John V. R. & Pat S. 2009. *The College Writer: A Guide to Thinking, Writing, and Researching (Third Edition).* Boston: Wadsworth Cengage Learning, 317.

use seems inevitable. The United States is a prime target for terrorism of this sort because the country has the largest, most efficiently raised food supply in the world. Destroying part of this supply would affect not only the United States but also all those countries with whom it trades. Because the United States is a prime target, it must act now to develop its defenses against agroterrorism. If the country waits until an attack happens, people may become ill, the overall economy could be damaged, and the agricultural economy may never recover.

写作实践 Writing Tasks

▶▶ **Complete the following opening paragraphs by using the opening strategies you have learned.**

(1) College study can be best defined as preparation for one's future life.

(2) Environment protection can only be achieved by raising people's awareness of it.

(3) Students should have the cultural awareness of the people who speak it if they want learn a language well.

(4) Children are suffering huge pressure which affects their physical and mental health.

(5) The scientific and technological advancement has brought many benefits to students' learning process.

Part 3 Five-paragraph Essay Writing

▶▶ **Provide supporting evidence by using different paragraph development strategies you have learned.**

(1) Topic sentence: Group learning brings many benefits to students.

　　Supporting details:

　　_____

　　_____

(2) Topic sentence: Communication technology is beneficial for people in many aspects.

　　Supporting details:

　　_____

　　_____

(3) Topic sentence: The constant exploration of the unknown promotes human being's continuous progress.

　　Supporting details:

　　_____

　　_____

(4) Topic sentence: The extensive international communication in many fields have exerted positive influences on China.

　　Supporting details:

　　_____

　　_____

(5) Topic sentence: Many Chinese traditional values and customs promote social and family harmony

　　Supporting details:

　　_____

　　_____

第 12 单元 修改
Unit 12 Revising

学习目标 Learning Objectives

1. 学习如何修改观点和文章结构；
2. 学习如何达到段落的统一性和连贯性。

课前任务 Pretask

回顾本书第二部分第 5 单元，学术文体风格中所讲的学术英语写作技巧（人称代词的使用、正式的语体风格等）。请找一篇英语短文，在小组讨论中对其写作风格进行评价并和其他小组成员相互交流。

引言 Introduction

初稿完成后是需要修改的，这是写作过程中必不可少的步骤。写作者要全方位地对初稿的进行修改，直到文章能够完全表达写作意图。首先，思考短文内容是否有趣、信息丰富、值得分享；其次，修改观点、结构；然后，检查修辞方法、语体风格以及语言表达等方面。

知识要点 Key Knowledge

12.1 修改观点和文章结构（Revise Ideas and Organization）

当修改初稿的内容时，要确保观点得到充分发展，文章结构清晰，即从观点句到整个论述过程要有很强的逻辑性。

12.1.1 清晰的观点（Clear Thesis）

确保整篇文章只围绕一个观点进行论述。下面的范例中原文缺少观点，修改后的观点更清晰明了。

范例[1]:

- Original passage (Lacks a thesis)

  Teen magazines are popular with young girls. These magazines contain a lot of how-to articles about self-image, fashion, and boy-girl relationships. Girls read them to get advice on how to act and how to look. Girls who don't really know what they want are the most eager readers.

- Revised version (Identifies a specific thesis statement)

  Adolescent girls often see teen magazines as handbooks on how to be teenagers. These magazines influence the ways they act and the ways they look. For girls who are unsure of themselves, these magazines can exert an enormous amount of influence. Unfortunately, the advice these magazines give about self-image, fashion, and boys may do more harm than good.

12.1.2 引言段的修改 (Revise the Opening Paragraph)

重新阅读引言段，思考以下问题：引言段的结构是否合理？引言段是否能吸引读者？是否清楚地表达了作者的观点并且指出了论述的主要内容？

范例[2]:

- Original opening (Lacks interest and direction)

  Bullying in schools is a huge problem that hurts both its victims and the people who practice it. Physical, verbal, and social bullying are all harmful in their own ways.

- Revised version (Effectively leads readers into the essay)

  A British prime minister once said, "Courage is fire, and bullying is smoke". If that is true, there is a lot of "smoke" present in most schools today. Bullying in schools is a huge problem that hurts both its victims and the people who practice it. Physical, verbal, and social bullying are all harmful in their own ways.

12.1.3 结束段的修改（Revise the Concluding Pragraph）

重新阅读结束段，思考以下问题：结尾段是否总结了文章的主要内容、观点，并且提

---

1 Randall V., Verne M., John V. R. & Pat S. 2009. *The College Writer: A Guide to Thinking, Writing, and Researching. (Third Edition).* Boston: Wadsworth Cengage Learning, 74.

2 兰甘. 2019. 美国大学英语写作. 广州：世界图书出版公司.

出了写作意义?

范例[1]:

- Original ending (Sketchy and flat)

  Learning about stress's causes and effects is an important first step that people must take. After that, they will be ready for the second step-learning how to manage life-threatening stress.

- Revised version (Effectively ends the writing)

  Because stress is so common, many people fail to recognize its potential danger. For example, Jan, the student described earlier, was certainly aware that she experienced stress while bustling through her busy morning. However, if she is like most college students, she wasn't aware that excessive stress could lead to serious illness and early death. Learning about stress's causes and effects is an important first step that they must take. After that, they will be ready for the second step-learning how to manage life-threatening stress.

12.2　主体段的修改（Revise the Middle Paragraphs）

初稿可能存在段落结构松散、主题发展不充分或不清楚等问题，修改时要注意段落的整体性、连贯性和完整性。

12.2.1　统一性（Check for unity）

一个具备统一性的段落是指这个段落中所有的细节内容都是围绕一个主题或一个写作目的。

1. 主题句（Topic sentence）

段落中包含主题的句子叫"主题句"，写作时应检查主题句表达是否清晰、具体，重点须突出。请参考下面这个主题句的写作公式：

Formula: A topic sentence = A limited topic + A specific feeling or thought about it

范例[2]:

- Studies now indicate that the inclination to take high risks (limited topic) may be hardwired into the brain, intimately linked to arousal and pleasure mechanisms, and may offer such a thrill that it functions like an addiction (a specific topic).

1　Randall V., Verne M., John V. R. & Pat S. 2009. *The College Writer: A Guide to Thinking, Writing, and Researching (Third Edition)*. Boston: Wadsworth Cengage Learning, 187.

2　Randall V., Verne M., John V. R. & Pat S. 2009. *The College Writer: A Guide to Thinking, Writing, and Researching (Third Edition)*. Boston: Wadsworth Cengage Learning, 279.

2. 支撑句（Supporting sentences）

段落中所有的支撑句都应该支持主题句，如果偏离了主题，可以参照下面的修改方法：

① 删除偏离主题的句子；

② 重写支撑句，使它们更清楚地支持主题句；

③ 修改主题句，使其与支撑句有紧密的逻辑关系。

3. 焦点一致性（Consistent focus）

包含不相关观点的段落缺乏统一性，使人难以理解，修改段落整体性时可以考虑下面几个问题：

① 段落的主题是否清晰？

② 每个句子都与主题相关吗？

③ 所有的支撑句是否按照一定的顺序排列？

范例：第 10 句和第 11 句脱离主题，删掉这两句话以后，整个段落就保持了统一性。

How to Prevent Cheating

Original paragraph (Lacks unity)

1. Instructors should take steps to prevent students from cheating on exams. 2. To begin with, instructors should stop reusing old tests. 3. A test that has been used even once is soon known on the student grapevine. 4. Students will check with their friends to find out, for example, what was on Dr. Thompson's biology final last term. 5. They may even manage to find a copy of the test itself, "accidentally" not turned in by a former student of Dr. Thompson's. 6. Instructors should also take some commonsense precautions at test time. 7. They should make students separate themselves-by at least one seat-during an exam, and they should watch the class closely. 8. The best place for the instructor to sit is in the rear of the room, so that a student is never sure if the instructor is looking at him or her. 9. Last of all, instructors must make it clear to students that there will be stiff penalties for cheating. <u>10. One of the problems with our school systems is a lack of discipline. 11. Instructors never used to give in to students' demands or put up with bad behavior, as they do today.</u> 12. Anyone caught cheating should immediately receive a zero for the exam. 13. A person even suspected of cheating should be forced to take an alternative exam in the instructor's office. 14. Because cheating is unfair to honest students, it should not be tolerated.

Revised version (Unified)

1. Instructors should take steps to prevent students from cheating on exams. 2. To begin with, instructors should stop reusing old tests. 3. A test that has been used even once is soon known on the student grapevine. 4. Students will check with their friends to find out, for example, what was on Dr. Thompson's biology final last term. 5. They may even manage to find a copy of the test itself, "accidentally" not turned in by a former student of Dr. Thompson's. 6. Instructors should also take some commonsense precautions at test time. 7. They should make students separate themselves-by at least one seat-during an exam, and they should watch the class closely. 8. The best place for the instructor to sit is in the rear of the room, so that a student is never sure if the instructor is looking at him or her. 9. Last of all, instructors must make it clear to students that there will be stiff penalties for cheating. 10. Anyone caught cheating should immediately receive a zero for the exam. 11. A person even suspected of cheating should be forced to take an alternative exam in the instructor's office. 12. Because cheating is unfair to honest students, it should not be tolerated.[①]

12.2.2 连贯性（Check for Coherence）

一个连贯的段落是流畅的，作者能够使每个句子通过重复和衔接等手段和其他句子连接起来。为了加强段落的连贯性，可以考虑以下两方面的问题：

1. 重复（Effective repetition）

在必要的地方使用重复的单词或同义词，也可以使用平行句型（包含多个相同语法结构的句子）来表达语句之间的关系。

2. 连接词（Clear transitions）

使用连接词有助于表达语句之间的连贯性。连接词可以用于表达地点和时间关系、比较和对比关系、强调、总结、递进或解释等。

范例[2]：

- Excessive **stress** is dangerous **not only** because of its link to serious illnesses, **but also** because of its very nature. In other words, **stress** is a nonspecific response: **Although**

---

1 兰甘. 2019. 美国大学英语写作. 广州：世界图书出版公司.

2 Randall V., Verne M., John V. R. & Pat S. 2009. *The College Writer: A Guide to Thinking, Writing, and Researching (Third Edition).* Boston: Wadsworth Cengage Learning, 187.

> stress may vary in degree, its nature is the same no matter what sort of threat is perceived. **In fact**, the threat doesn't even have to be real! As long as a person perceives a threat, he or she will experience stress. **For example**, someone who is afraid of poisonous spiders may undergo great stress even when in the presence of a harmless spider. **In addition**, the nonspecific nature of stress works the other way: Someone who is in real danger, but doesn't perceive the danger, will experience no stress. **Finally**, stress's nonspecific nature makes stress particularly dangerous for those people who perceive threats very readily. These individuals experience stress more commonly-and often more intensely-than others.

The words and phrases below can help you tie together words, phrases, sentences, and paragraphs.

Transitions and Lingking Words[1]

Words used to show location:	above, across, against, along, among, around, away, from, behind, below, beneath, besides, between, beyon, by, down, in back of, in front of, inside, into, near, off, on top of, outside, over, throughout, to the right, under
Words used to show time:	about, after, afterward, as soon as, at, before, during, finally, first, immediately, later, meanwhile, next, next week, second, soon, then, third, today, tomorrow, until, when, yesterday, formerly, previously, prior to, to begin with, thereafter, subsequently, presently, eventually
Words used to compare things (Show similarities):	also, as, in the same way, like, likewise, similarly, in the like manner, to have in common, accordingly, correspondingly
Words used to contrast things (Show Differences):	although, but, even though, however, on the other hand, otherwise, still, yet, nevertheless, otherwise, in contrast to, in the opposition to, on the opposite side
Words used to emphasize a point:	again, even, particularly, to emphasize, for this reason, in fact, to repeat, truly,

---

[1] Randall V., Verne M., John V. R. & Pat S. 2009. *The College Writer: A Guide to Thinking, Writing, and Researching (Third Edition).* Boston: Wadsworth Cengage Learning, 85.

续表

Words used to conclude or summarize:	all in all, as a result, finally, in conclusion, in summary, last, therefore, to sum up,
Words used to add information:	additionally, again, along with, also, and, another, as well, besides, equally important, finally, for example, for instance, in addition, likewise, next, second
Words used to clarify:	for instance, in other words, put another way, that is
Words used to show cause and effect:	so, thus, hence, as a result of, have an effect on, due to owing to thanks to the cause of, onsequently, the consequence of, so that, seeing that, for fear that, accordingly

12.2.3 完整性（Check for Completeness）

一个段落中的支撑句应该支持和扩展段落主旨，如果段落不完整，须添加一些细节内容，包括 facts、anecdotes、analyses、statistics、quotations、explanations、examples definitions、summaries。作者应该根据文章类型和写作目的添加细节内容。如下文范例中的原文缺少细节内容，改写后的段落增加了例子及分析，加强了完整性。

- Original paragraph (Lacks completeness)

  One of the most immediate results of prolonged stress is a decrease in the body's natural immune function. The release of cortisol into the bloodstream inhibits a protective hormone released during the immune response and thereby suppresses immune reactions.

- Revised version (Full development)

  One of the most immediate results of prolonged stress is a decrease in the body's natural immune function. The release of cortisol into the bloodstream inhibits a protective hormone released during the immune response and thereby suppresses immune reactions. During periods of stress, the immune system becomes compromised, and the body experiences increased susceptibility to disease. For example, some studies have proven that when medical students prepare for board exams, they experience more stress and get sick more often than when they prepare for less stressful exams.[1]

---

[1] Randall V., Verne M., John V. R. & Pat S. 2009. *The College Writer: A Guide to Thinking, Writing, and Researching (Third Edition)*. Boston: Wadsworth Cengage Learning, 186.

写作实践 Writing Tasks

▶▶ **Choose one of the following topics and write a five-paragraph essay.**

(1) Can physical bookstores survive in the digital age?

(2) What's behind Chinese parents' anxiety about education ?

(3) Is it time to ease the burden on students?

(4) Will online education replace traditional learning?

(5) Is the development of social media a positive one or a negative one?

▶▶ **After you finish your first draft you should revise it based on the following thinking questions of assessing you own writing.**

(1) Does the title announce the subject of your text and give some sense of what you have to say?

(2) Does the beginning grab readers' attention? If so, how does it do so? Does it give enough information about the topic? Offer necessary background information?

(3) What is your thesis?

(4) Does the essay have a clear pattern of organization? Does each body paragraph relate to the thesis and support or develop that point? Do any paragraphs or sentences stray from your focus?

(5) What reasons and evidence do you give to support your thesis?

(6) What transitions help readers move from idea to idea and paragraph to paragraph?

(7) Does the ending leave readers thinking about your main point? Is there another way of concluding the essay that would sharpen your focus?

第四部分 写作备考

Part 4　Writing for Tests

内容提要
Preview

　　第四部分包括四个单元，介绍大学英语四、六级考试，雅思考试、托福考试和研究生入学英语考试写作部分的评分原则、标准以及写作特点和过程。第 13 单元为大学英语四、六级写作；第 14 单元为雅思写作；第 15 单元为托福写作；第 16 单元为考研英语写作。

第13单元 大学英语四、六级写作

Unit 13 Writing for CET-4 and CET-6

学习目标 Learning Objectives

1. 了解大学英语四、六级考试作文的评分标准和原则；
2. 掌握大学英语四、六级考试作文的写作步骤。

课前任务 Pretask

请给下面两个考试题目写出文章提纲。

1. Directions: For this part, you are allowed 30 minutes to write an essay on "Why should students be encouraged to develop effective communication skills?". You should write at least 150 words but no more than 200 words.

2. Directions: For this part, you are allowed 30 minutes to write an essay entitled "Should Food Be Banned on the Subway?". You can cite examples to illustrate your points. You should write at least 120 words but no more than 180 words.

引言 Introduction

《大学英语四六级考试大纲》要求考生能够运用英语进行短文写作，且思想表达准确，意义连贯，无语法错误。具体考核要求是：思想表达方面，考生能够表达中心思想、观点态度及重要信息；篇章组织方面，考生能够围绕所给的题目叙述、议论或描述，突出重点，并能够连贯地组句成段、组段成篇；语言运用方面，考生能够运用恰当的词汇、正确的语法、合适的句子结构，以及对比、原因、结果、程度、目的等衔接手段表达句间关系。

知识要点 Key Knowledge

13.1 评分原则（Scoring Principles）

① 作文题采用总体评分方法。阅卷人员首先就总体印象给出奖励分，而不是按语言的错误点扣分。

② 从内容和语言两个方面对作文进行综合评判。作文应表达题目所规定的内容，阅卷人员既要考虑作文是否切题，是否充分表达思想，也要考虑语言是否清楚且合适地表达了思想，也就是要考虑语言错误是否会造成理解障碍。

③ 避免趋中倾向。该给高分的给高分，包括满分（15分）；该给低分的给低分，包括零分，不应只给中间的几种分数。

④ 阅卷标准共分五等：2分、5分、8分、11分及14分。阅卷人员根据阅卷标准，对照样卷评分，若认为与某一分数（如8分）相似，即定为该分数（即8分）；若认为稍优或稍劣于该分数，则可加1分（即9分）或减1分（即7分），一般不加或减半分。

13.2 评分标准（Scoring Criteria）

① 白卷——作文与题目毫不相关，或只有几个孤立的词且无法表达思想，则给0分。

② 2分——条理不清，思路紊乱，语言支离破碎，大部分句子均有错误，且多数为严重错误。

③ 5分——基本切题。思想表达得不清楚，连贯性差，有较多的严重语言错误。

④ 8分——基本切题。有些地方思想表达得不够清楚，文字勉强连贯，语言错误相当多，其中有一些是严重错误。

⑤ 11分——切题。思想表达得清楚，文字连贯，但有少量语言错误。

⑥ 14分——切题。思想表达得清楚，文字通顺、连贯，基本上无语言错误，仅有个别小错。

⑦ 字数不足应酌情扣分，题目中给出的主题句、起始句、结束句，均不得计入所写字数，规定的内容未写全者，按比例扣分。

13.3 实战分析（Analysis of Writing Practice）

13.3.1 图表式作文（Writings with Diagrams and Pictures）

图表式作文包括很多种类：折线图、柱状图、点阵图、饼状图、数据表格、图画（如漫画、卡通）等。

范例：

图 13-1　2015 年 12 月大学英语六级真题

Directions: For this part, you are allowed 30 minutes to write a short essay based on the picture below. You should focus on **the harm caused by misleading information online.** You are required to write at least 150 words but no more than 200 words.

写作步骤：审题 — 立意 — 提纲 — 初稿 — 修改

这个范例的**审题**和**立意**是相对容易的，作文指令给定了写作的立场和论点，而且漫画中画中人的那句："I just feel unfortunate to live in a world with so much misleading information"和作文的指令是相呼应的，目的是引导考生分析和论证网上误导性的信息带来的危害。

范例提纲：

The harm caused by misleading information online

Opening paragraph:

Describe the issue depicted in the cartoon: misleading online information is ubiquitous.

Advance the argument: misleading online information brings severe damages to the society.

Body paragraph：

Topic sentence A: Deceptive news or tips travel fast online, and worse still, they may shadow our routine life or even hinder the progress of our society.

Topic sentence B: If the misleading news is not corrected soon, there may be a trust crisis between individuals and the government.

Ending paragraph：

Suggestions to prevent misleading online information and expectation for the future.

请按照提纲完成初稿后，对照表13-1修改。

表13-1 修改对照表

内容	• 是否按照题目要求正确理解并描述漫画揭示的现象； • 论点是否和题目要求一致； • 论据是否具体而充实，数量是够充分； • 结论是否自然而圆满。
结构	• 文章是否至少分开头、主体、结论三段，段落的组织和开展是否使用了清晰的方法，如例证、对比、因果分析等； • 主体段是否有两到三个不同的主题句（主体段是否根据论证的不同角度、层次，提出和排列主题句及相关支撑细节），主题是否一致，是否能够共同支撑文章的论点； • 句子之间的衔接、过渡是否自然和符合逻辑，是否使用过渡和衔接的词汇。
语言	• 用词是否准确、恰当、生动、具体、地道，句子是否简洁、完整、充分地表达了语义，句式是否富有变化，符合修辞和语法规则； • 是否有以下常见错误：拼写错误、单复数错误、a/the 的滥用或者省略、时态错误、词语搭配错误、指代错误、人称前后不一致、生僻词、俚语或口语化语言、陈词滥调、故作高深的表达方式等； • 是否有以下常见句子错误：语义前后矛盾或者违背常识和逻辑、句子结构前后不平行、主谓不一致、粘连句、主从句倒置、句式杂糅、修饰语悬垂、句子结构残缺等。

范例分析：

The Harm Caused by Misleading Information Online

It is true that the internet has brought us great convenience and efficiency（第一句以背景信息引入话题）. However, just as shown in the cartoon, as the data grows at an exponential rate, the severity of misleading information arises（指出漫画所传达的观点）.

Deceptive news or tips travel fast online, and worse still, they may shadow our routine life or even hinder the progress of our society（主体段的第一个分论点）. Lack of enough consideration and independent thinking, people are easily misled by false information which always appears in bulk on the web page. Some will change their normal life plans to deal with the false information; a few may even go panic and violate social security rules and break laws because of the deceptive news or tips（针对第一个分论点的分析）. Moreover, if the misleading news is not corrected soon, there may be a trust crisis between individuals and the governments（主体段的第二个分论点）. For example, the nuclear leakage in Japan in 2011 has caused great panic in Eastern China, where thousands of people rushed to purchase salt after the rumor that salt can prevent radiation went around and ended up disturbing the domestic market. This chaos could be avoided if the government clarify the false news on time（例证第二个分论点）.

To prevent misleading information from spreading, governments should set up laws to regulate online news while individuals need to judge independently. Only when they work together would the harm of false information be diminished（结尾提出建议和忠告）.

13.3.2 命题式作文（Writings with a Given Topic）

命题式作文虽题材广泛，但一般分为两类：一类是在题目中给定文章的论点、立场、态度，考生只需要对给定的观点进行分析、论证并得出结论即可（如例题1）；另一类是题目给出一个开放式的问题或者有争议的观点，需要考生自主选择立场，确定观点，然后再分析、论证并得出结论（如例题2）。

例题1：2018年12月大学英语六级作文真题

Directions: For this part, you are allowed 30 minutes to write an essay on **How to balance work and leisure.** You should write at least 150 words but no more than 200 words.

范文分析：

How to Balance Work and Leisure

Just as the old saying goes, "All work and no play makes Jack a dull boy", which illustrates the importance and necessity of keeping a balance between work and leisure（第一句引用谚语，引出话题）. However, in today's fast-paced work culture, it is difficult for most people to successfully maintain a good balance between the two（指出题目给定的问题）.

As for me, some tips can contribute to achieving the balance（主体段的主题句给出具体建议，以解决工作和休闲平衡的问题）. First of all, you should develop efficient working habits, because only in this way can you squeeze out some leisure time（提出第一条建议）. It requires you to devote your full attention to the task at hand and complete daily work efficiently（对第一条建议的分析）. Second, in order to relieve the fatigue and stress, it is vital to schedule one thing that you are interested in each day and set aside some time for relaxation（提出第二条建议，同时做了分析）. Last but not least, for those workaholics, please keep in mind that you shouldn't feel guilty when you spend time on personal leisure, for entertainment is also a

part of life（第三条专门给"工作狂"的建议）.

To conclude, work and leisure complement each other（一句话总结主体段的建议）, so when you get tired and bored with your daily routine, try to take some time off to relax yourself（最后提醒读者要保持平衡，结束全文）.

例题 2：2017 年 6 月大学英语六级作文真题

Directions: Suppose you are asked to give advice on whether to attend a vocational college or a university, write an essay to state your opinion. You are required to write at least 150 words but no more than 200 words.

范例分析：

With the flourish of education industry, modern students are faced with more alternatives to continue their further education（通过背景信息，引入话题）. Both attending a vocational college or a university serves as two main options for the high school graduates（指出题目给出的问题）. In terms of which to choose and what to be taken into consideration, I shall advise as follows（表明目的是解决问题并给出建议）.

Primarily, self-orientation matters the most when it comes to a issue like this（提出第一条的观点也是主体段的第一个主题句：解决此类问题的原则是看自己的倾向。其实这样的观点比较中庸，但是符合中国人的思维习惯，温和的建议更能让人接受。但完全按照题目二选一给建议，更符合英语思维，立场鲜明，易于说服别人）. Obviously, the main task of vocational college is cultivating human resource with practical capability. Instead, university serves as the cradle of academic researchers in different areas（分析职业学校和综合性大学的主要区别）. Therefore, being aware of your self-expectation with a clear future blueprint lays a foundation for this important decision（给出具体的建议）.

Apart from what has been mentioned above, personal interest also plays a key role in it（提出第二条的观点也是主体段的第二个主题句）. For both passion and motivation are derived from interest, which not only decide how far you can reach academically and professionally but also how happy and fulfilled you will be（给出支撑的理据）.

To sum up, a clear recognition of self orientation and personal interest will decide whether you will tick the box of vocational college or university（重申论点）. Only in this way can we get the most out of the further education（强调论点的意义，结束全文）.

第四部分 写作备考
Part 4 Writing for Tests

写作实践 Writing Tasks

▶▶ 图表作文：（Writings with Diagrams and Pictures）

Directions: For this part, you are allowed 30 minutes to write an essay based on the chart below. You should start your essay with a brief description of the chart and comment on China's achievements in higher education. You should write at least 150 words but no more than 200 words.

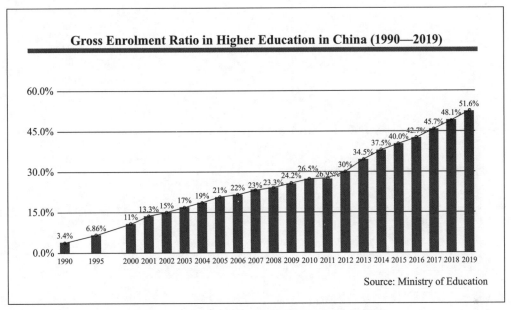

图 13-2　2021 年 6 月大学英语六级作文真题

▶▶ 给定论点的命题作文：（Writings with a Given Thesis）

Directions：For this part, you are allowed 30 minutes to write an essay on why students should be encouraged to develop effective communication skills. You should write at least 150 words but no more than 200 words.

2020 年 12 月大学英语六级真题

▶▶ 开放式问题的命题作文[1]：（Writings Without a Given Thesis）

Directions: For this part, you are allowed 30 minutes to write an essay entitled "Should Food Be Banned on the Subway?". You can cite examples to illustrate your points. You should write at least 120 words but no more than 180 words.

1　朱娜．2018．大学英语四级写作教程．北京：首都经济贸易大学出版社．

125

第 14 单元　雅思写作
Unit 14　Writing for IELTS

学习目标 Learning Objectives

1. 了解雅思写作的评分标准和原则；
2. 掌握雅思作文的写作步骤。

课前任务 Pretask

请给下面两个考试题目写出文章提纲。

1. You should spend about 40 minutes on this task.

Write about the following topic:

Nowadays, the trend of fashion changes very rapidly, and gradually people become the slaves to it. Some people think that a person should choose comfortable clothes, which he or she likes, regardless of fashion. Do you agree? Write an essay to state your opinion.

Give reasons for your answer and include any relevant examples from your own knowledge or experience.

Write at least 250 words.

2. You should spend about 40 minutes on this task.

Write about the following topic:

Some information in films, books and on the internet has bad influence on young people and even on society. What are these bad influences and what should we do to prevent them?

Give reasons for your answer and include any relevant examples from your own knowledge or experience.

Write at least 250 words.

引言 Introduction

雅思写作要求考生在 60 分钟内完成两篇作文 Task 1 和 Task 2。Task 1 部分，以移民为主的普通培训类（General Training Module，简称 G 类）和以留学为主的学术类（Academic Module，简称 A 类）的试题类型不同。Task 1 的考试时间为 20 分钟，考生要写一篇至少 150 词的作文，其中 G 类要求写一封信来询问某方面信息或阐释某种状况，而 A 类则要针对一个或多个互相关联的图表、图解或表格，对信息或数据进行描述。Task 2 的考试时间为 40 分钟，考生要写一篇至少 250 词的议论文。在 Task 2 部分，G 类和 A 类的考试内容和形式非常相似，考生都要根据某一开放性或者争议性的问题、现象、观点发表个人意见，并用论据论证自己观点的合理性。

知识要点 Key Knowledge

14.1 评分标准与原则（Scoring Criteria and Principles）

雅思写作部分的评分范围为 0~9 分，评分人员按照以下标准和原则评分。

Task 1

① 写作任务完成情况（Task achievement）。完成写作任务是指考生能用规定的字数达到写作要求。G 类写作要求考生能够清晰表达写信目的，通过书信实现交际功能和效果，写作风格、格式、语气要得体；A 类写作要求考生能够涵盖写作任务的各项要求，能通过仔细读图确切地提取关键信息，并用语言清晰全面地描述这些信息，且能详细分析、说明图表主要特征，不得遗漏某个重要特征，否则按比例扣分。

② 衔接与连贯（Coherence and cohesion）。写作信息和观点组织要连贯且有逻辑性，论证过程要清楚，文章通篇具有延续性，能够恰当使用衔接手段。

③ 词汇（Lexical resource）。词汇是指考生在写作中体现的词汇量和准确度。词汇使用范围广，从日常生活词汇到学术词汇，考生应能自如、灵活地使用多样化的词汇来表达思想，且用词准确、恰当，对语体和搭配掌握良好。

④ 语法范围和准确性（Grammatical range and accuracy）。语法范围是指考生能用多种语法和句型结构来进行写作，而准确性是指所用的语法或句型结构是正确的，能够使用多种复杂语法结构，句式变化多样，基本准确无误。

Task 2

① 对写作任务的回应（Task response）。作文符合题目的所有要求：文章切题，立场清晰明确；能够提出、引申并支持主要观点；观点鲜明，论证充分。

② 衔接与连贯性（coherence and cohesion）。写作信息和观点组织有序、且有逻辑性；全文布局合理，有延续性；衔接手段使用合理，分段恰当。

③ 词汇（Lexical resource）。词汇使用丰富，有一定的准确性和灵活性；能使用日常词汇范围以外的词汇，对语体和搭配有所掌握。

④ 语法范围和准确性（Grammatical range and accuracy）。语法结构的使用广泛、准确而灵活；句式变化多样，基本准确无误。

14.2 实战分析（Analysis of Writing Practice）

Task 1[1]:

You should spend 20 minutes on this task.

The charts below give information about travelling to and from the UK, and about the most popular countries for UK residents to visit.

Summarize the information by selecting and reporting the main features, and make comparisons where relevant.

Write at least 150 words.

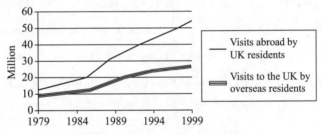

图 14-1　Visits to and from the UK

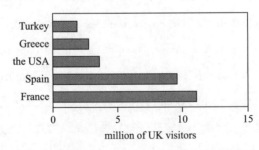

图 14-2　Most popular countries visited by UK residents in 1999

审题：雅思图表作文中的图表数量不一，从一张到六张都有，但一般一张或者两张图表居多。不管有几张图表，考生主要从对象、时间、数字变化读取图表的特征。例如，图

---

1 杨凡. 雅思写作官方题库大全. 北京：电子工业出版社.

14-1 的折线图是出国游的英国人数量和到英国入境游的外国人数量,时间是 1979—1999 年,人数是从 0~6,000 万;图 14-2 柱状图有五个对象:土耳其、希腊、美国、西班牙、法国,时间是 1999 年,人数是 0~1,500 万。

立意:这两张表格之间虽然有一定关系,但不具有可比性,所以应独立描述。

提纲:三段式作文。第一段总述,分别用一句话总结两张图表的内容;第二段详细描述第一张图表的两个对象在 1979—1999 年人数上的变化,并且针对变化的不同特点进行比较总结;第三段详细描述 1999 年,在五个对象国中,英国游客人数的不同,并总结数字差异体现的特点,应尤其注意最小值、最大值和平均值所体现的特点。

范文分析:

> The line graph shows the information about travelling to and from the UK for 20 years to 1999. The bar chart compares the five most popular countries for UK residents in 1999.(第一段总述,分别用一句话总结两张图表的内容)
>
> We can see from the line graph that there was a slight increase in the number of visits abroad by UK residents from 12 million in 1979 to 20 million in 1985. However, after that, the number rose sharply until 1999, peaking at a little over 50 million. During the same time period, there was a slow growth in the number of visits to the UK by overseas residents. From 1979 to 1999, the number of visits abroad was larger than that of visits to the UK.(第二段详细描述第一张图表的两个对象在 1979—1999 年人数上的变化,并且针对变化的不同特点进行比较总结)
>
> It can be seen from the bar chart that France was the most popular country for UK residents in 1999. Spain had the second largest number of UK visitors in the five countries. Although the number to the USA was much smaller than that to Spain, it was slightly larger than that to Greece. Turkey was the least popular country among the five countries. In 1999, about 2.5 million of UK travelers had been to Turkey.(第三段详细描述 1999 年,在五个对象国中,英国游客人数的不同,并总结数字差异所体现的特点,尤其注意最小值、最大值和平均值所体现的特点)

Task 2

这一部分的命题作文绝大多数是辩论式题目,主要考察考生的思辨逻辑和批判性思维;但偶尔也会有非辩论式题目,主要考察考生分析问题和解决问题的思维能力。辩论式题目提问题的方式主要分两类：一类是提出一个有争议性的话题，隐含正反两种立场和观点，询问考生意见（如例题1）；另一类是对一个有争议的话题明确给出正反两方的立场和观点，要求考生先讨论两方观点，再提出自己的观点（如例题2）。不论是哪类题目，考生首先要考虑的是立场，一般有五种可选择的立场（见表14-1）。

表14-1 五种可选立场

1	2	3	4	5
完全支持	完全反对	支持反对各占50%	部分支持	部分反对
极少选择	极少选择	不选择	可选	可选

一般极少数考生会选择完全支持和完全反对的立场，因为绝大多数情况下，正反观点都有一定的道理，"一边倒"的立场给人感觉不成熟、不理性、不客观。考生一般也不会选择支持反对各占50%的立场，这种立场试图两边都讨好，结果立场模糊，缺乏独立观点，不知所云。部分支持或者部分反对的立场显得客观、理性，一方面承认对方立场和观点的存在有其合理性，另一方面更多地指出其不合理的地方，进而论证自己立场和观点的正当性。

例题1

辩论式题目：

You should spend about 40 minutes on this task.

Write about the following topic:

Now many people are forgetting their history and culture, so some people suggest that we should encourage people to wear their traditional clothing every day. Do you agree?

Give reasons for your answer and include any relevant examples from your own knowledge or experience.

Write at least 250 words.

审题：题目中的观点"为了让人们记住历史和文化，有人建议应该鼓励人们每天穿着传统服装"有点极端。

立意：考生应该采取部分否定的立场。

提纲：第一段开篇引入题目中的观点，也就是反方观点，表明自己的立场。第二段先承认反方观点的合理性，再提出自己的观点：传统服装不适合现代生活和工作。第三段用证据支撑自己的观点的正当性，一方面快节奏的工作和生活需要不同种类和功能的现代服装；另一方面每天穿传统服装并不能起到保护传统文化的作用。第四段建议通过教育方式铭记历史和文化。第五段重申自己的立场和观点，再次有条件地承认反方观点的合理性。

范文分析：

Some people suggest that we should wear our traditional clothing every day, since many people are forgetting history and culture（开篇第一段引入题目中观点，也是反方观点）. As far as I am concerned, this proposal seems a bit absurd and ridiculous（表明自己的立场）.

Nobody should ignore and forget our brilliant history and gorgeous culture. Without doubt, traditional clothing is part of our cultural heritage as well as a symbol of our civilization. In many people's minds, the traditional clothing is elegant and graceful, with Which I am totally in agreement（第二段承认反方观点的合理性）. But it doesn't mean that old-fashioned dresses are suitable for our work and life in the present-day society（再提出自己观点：传统服装不适合现代生活和工作）.

We are living in a brand new era, full of challenges and opportunities.（主体部分第一段，用证据支撑自己的观点的正当性）With the tempo of people's living and working speeding up, people have to hurry up to work on weekdays, and go outdoors to exercise or relax themselves on weekends. Therefore, there are different sorts of clothes for different functions and occasions（证据一：快节奏的工作和生活需要不同种类和功能的现代服装）. Furthermore, it is a superficial way to encourage people to wear traditional clothes with the aim of remembering history and culture. I don't think it works as some advocates expect（证据二：每天穿传统服装并不能起到保护传统文化的作用）.

The campaign to make sure not to forget our history and culture calls for long-term efforts（主体部分第二段的主题句，换个角度继续论证自己观点的合理性）. People can be better cultivated through comprehensive education in history and culture（建议通过教育方式铭记历史和文化）. When people are learning more about history and culture, their pride and curiosity will be aroused. I believe that this kind of education will play a crucial role in keeping people remembering the past and benefit the future generations. Moreover, we should adopt a correct attitude towards the past, that is to say, to absorb the essence and reject the dross.

In a word, I can hardly share the proposal that people should be encouraged to wear the traditional clothing every day in order to preserve history and culture（结尾重申自己立场和观点）. However, on some special occasions, such as during Chinese traditional festivals, it is acceptable to wear traditional costumes, which adds colour to the festivity,（再次有条件地承认反方观点的合理性，证明自己思考问题的客观性和全面性）.

例题 2

辩论式题目：

You should spend about 40 minutes on this task.

Write about the following topic:

In some countries, advertisers persuade children to buy some goods, such as snacks, toys, and other goods. As for this phenomenon, parents object such practice on children. But some advertisers claim that there is useful information in these advertisements.

Discuss both these views and give your own opinions.

Give reasons for your answer and include any relevant examples from your own knowledge or experience.

Write at least 250 words.

审题：题目中明确列出了辩论双方的立场和观点：广告方和家长方，要求考生予以讨论并给出自己的立场和观点。

立意：考生首先要明确自己的立场，更倾向于哪一方，然后再展开讨论。

提纲：第一段开篇引入话题，明确立场，站在家长这一边；第二段分析广告对有孩子的家庭带来不良的影响；第三段分析广告方的辩护理由，并进行反驳；第四段重申自己的观点，并有条件承认某些公益类广告对儿童教育的合理性。

范文分析：

It is a common phenomenon that an overwhelming number of advertisements regard children as the target group, and persuade them, especially their parents, to buy clothes, toys and even some luxuries（开篇以背景信息引入话题）. Urgently, these advertising means need a thorough examination as for its justification（明确立场，站在父母这一边，表明观点）.

There is no doubt that such advertisements exert a repercussion on children's family（主体部分第一段的主题句，指出广告对孩子带来不良的影响）. Generally speaking, children can influence the family's purchasing orientation, which is best illustrated in Chinese families where the family planning is strictly pursued. Due to this national policy in China, adults are unwilling to have more kids, so children are usually spoilt. Their children's every need, even unreasonable ones, will be satisfied. Under such circumstances, some manufacturerstake advantage of children's inexperience and impulsion, designing fancy advertisements to draw their attention and even cheat kids, which will drag families under unbearable economic burden

(例证支撑主题句).

　　The side representing the interests of manufacturers and advertising agencies, of course, insists that there must be advertisement belonging to youngsters（主体部分第二段，指出广告方的辩护理据）. According to their understanding, children can benefit from those specific advertisements just as adults do, and otherwise it is unfair in that they have no other channels to know any commodity information concerning their particular world. As for me, however, the main responsibility children assume at their age group is to acquire as much knowledge as possible, so in the future they can make a substantial contribution to society. If what they pay attention to is about fashion, then their learning efficiency is really doubted（反驳广告方的辩护理据）.

　　My view is that in view of children's vulnerable mentality and weighty responsibility, advertisements for children should be limited（结尾段重申自己的立场和观点）. Even if we allow some ones, they must be public service advertisements arousing concern for social vulnerable groups rather than encouraging buying（有条件地承认某些公益类广告对儿童教育的合理性）.

非思辨式题目：

You should spend about 40 minutes on this task.

Write about the following topic:

The traffic jam is a problem in big cities. What causes the problem? Make some recommendations.

Give reasons for your answer and include any relevant examples from your own knowledge or experience.

Write at least 250 words.

审题：非思辨式题目一般要求考生对某一问题的原因、影响、结果等方面进行分析，然后给出解决问题的合理化建议。

立意：考生应在文章的开头段按照要求表明自己的立场、态度和观点等，以统摄全文，使全文主题一致，思路连贯。

提纲：第一段开篇以今夕对照引入话题，提出本文的主要目的；第二段在主体部分第一段分析第一个原因，城市人口数量上升必然导致交通拥堵；第三段主体部分第二段分析第二个原因，私家车太多挤占公交车的空间；第四段主体部分第三段分析第三个原因，部分司机、骑车人和行人不遵守交规；第五段结尾段从三个角度提出合理建议。

范文分析：

In the past, there were not so many motor vehicles on the road and we enjoyed a very good traffic condition. However, in recent years, along with the rapid development of urban traffic, certain problems have arisen, one of which is the traffic jam. It has become common to see passengers and drivers having to wait in long lines of buses and cars during the rush hours (开篇通过今夕对照引入话题). It is imperative that we pinpoint the causes of this disturbing problem (提出本文的主要目的是分析交通拥堵的原因).

First of all, there are an increasing number of residents living in big cities (主体部分，第一段主题句说明第一个原因，城市人口数量上升必然导致交通拥堵). Every year, men and women flood into big cities because there are more job opportunities. These people need to go out to work or study. No matter what kind of transportation they take, traffic volume will inevitably rise (事实和逻辑分析支撑第一个原因).

Another reason is that there are too many private cars and not enough public buses (主体部分，第二段主题句说明第二个原因，私家车太多挤占公交车的空间). As a result of the increasing income, most families can afford their own cars and some of them even have two cars. However, in most cases, a car carries only one or two people, while it occupies almost half the space a bus does (因果分析支撑第二个原因).

In addition, many people, such as drivers, pedestrians and cyclists, disobey traffic rules (主体部分，第三段主题句说明第三个原因，部分司机、骑车人和行人不遵守交规). For example, some people drive after drinking, some run the red light, and some surpass the speed limit. All these things undoubtedly worsen the already severe situation (举例支撑第三个原因).

In view of the seriousness of this problem, effective measures must be taken before things get worse (结尾段从三个角度提出合理建议). First, there is a need for the government to try its best to narrow the gap between big cities and rural areas. Second, we should give priority to the development of public transportation and impose restrictions on the use of private cars in urban areas. What is more, it is the government's responsibility to organize activities to promote public awareness of the importance of obeying traffic regulations (三个建议合情合理，值得借鉴).

写作实践 Writing Tasks

图表式作文[1]：(Writings with Diagrams and Pictures)

You should spend about 20 minutes on this task.

The charts below show what UK graduates and postgraduate students who did not go into full-time work after leaving college in 2008.

Summarize the information by selecting and reporting the main features, and make comparisons where relevant.

Write at least 150 words.

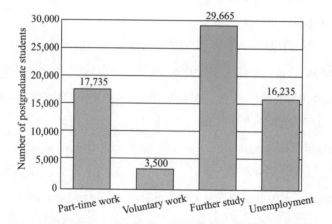

图 14-3　Destinations of UK graduates (excluding full-time work) 2008

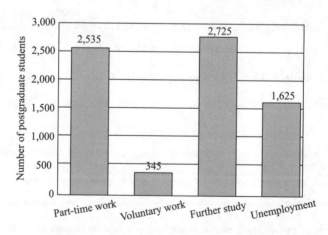

图 14-4　Destinations of UK postgraduates (excluding full-time work) 2008

1　刘薇. 2018. 雅思写作全薇机经. 北京：石油工业出版社.

▶▶ 辩论式命题作文 1：(Writings with a Debable Topic 1)

You should spend about 40 minutes on this task.

Write about the following topic:

Nowadays, the trend of fashion changes very rapidly, and gradually people become the slaves to it. Some people think that a person should choose comfortable clothes, which he or she likes, regardless of fashion. Do you agree? Write an essay to state your opinion.

Give reasons for your answer and include any relevant examples from your own knowledge or experience.

Write at least 250 words.

▶▶ 辩论式命题作文 2：(Writings with a Debable Topic 2)

You should spend about 40 minutes on this task.

Write about the following topic:

Technological development causes a lot of environmental problems. As for the issue, some people think a simple life style can protect the environment while others argue that technology itself can solve it. Discuss both sides and give your own opinion.

Give reasons for your answer and include any relevant examples from your own knowledge or experience.

Write at least 250 words.

▶▶ 非辩论命题作文：(Writings with a Given Topic)

You should spend about 40 minutes on this task.

Write about the following topic:

Some information in films, books and on the Internet has bad influence on young people and even on society. What are these bad influences and what should we do to prevent them?

Give reasons for your answer and include any relevant examples from your own knowledge or experience.

Write at least 250 words.

第 15 单元　托福写作
Unit 15　Writing for TOEFL

学习目标 Learning Objectives

1. 了解托福考试作文的评分标准和原则；
2. 掌握托福考试作文的写作步骤。

课前任务 Pretask

请给下面的考试题目写出文章提纲。

Directions: Read the question below. You have 30 minutes to plan, write and revise your essay. Typically, an effective response will contain a minimum of 300 words.

Question: Do you agree or disagree with the following statement? Face-to-face communication is better than other types of communication, such as letters, email, or telephone calls.

Use specific reasons and details to support your answer.

引言 Introduction

托福写作分为两种形式：综合写作（Integrated writing）和独立写作（Independent writing），考查考生的学术英语写作能力，考生必须能用清晰、有条理的方式陈述学术观点。

知识要点 Key Knowledge

15.1 基本信息（Basic Information）

表 15-1 基本信息

	综合写作	独立写作
形式	相关听力 + 短文阅读 + 写作	议论文写作
内容	总结听力内容和短文内容之间的关系	针对可选择性的、有争议的话题发表观点
时间	20 分钟	30 分钟
字数	150~225 词	不少于 300 词
三档分制	满分 5 分 Good: 4~5 分 Fair: 2.5~3.5 分 Limited: 1~2 分	满分 5 分 Good: 4~5 分 Fair: 2.5~3.5 分 Limited: 1~2 分
30 分制	满分 30 分 Good: 24~30 分 Fair: 17~23 分 Limited: 1~14 分	满分 30 分 Good: 24~30 分 Fair: 17~23 分 Limited: 1~14 分

15.2 考察要点：（Key Points for Testing）

综合写作要求：

① 对听到和读到的材料做提纲式笔记，在写作前利用笔记组织信息；

② 准确地从原文材料中总结、释义和引用信息；

③ 写出听到的信息与读到的信息之间的相互关系；

独立写作要求（考生需要依据自身的知识和经历表达并支持一种观点）：

① 确定中心思想（观点或者论点），以及支持该观点的两到三个次论点和相应的论据；

② 组织论文，利用提纲列举要点；

③ 利用一定的论证方式，如对比、推论、例证、定义、程序等详细地展开论述，使文章主题一致，论证充分有力；

④ 使用有条理、符合逻辑的方式表达信息；

⑤ 运用有效的连接词（过渡词组）来连接内容，帮助读者厘清脉络；

⑥ 正确和地道地运用语法和词汇，做到有效表达；

⑦ 遵循拼写、标点和格式的语言惯例。

15.3 综合写作评分标准（Scoring Criteria for Integrated Writing）

表 15-2　综合写作评分标准

分数	任务描述
5	可以成功地找出听力讲座中的重要信息，明确这些信息与阅读短文中关键信息的相关性，并能连贯且准确地呈现出来。语言组织结构清晰，偶尔有错误但不会导致内容不准确或者前后不连贯。
4	可以很好地找出听力讲座中重要信息，明确这些信息与阅读短文中关键信息的相关性，并连贯且准确地呈现出来。但在获取某些内容或与阅读短文中要点之间的相关性方面可能存在小的遗漏，不准确或不精确。有一些常见的、明显的、小的语言错误，这些错误导致部分内容不清晰或者不连贯。
3	包含一些听力讲座中的重要信息，表达了与阅读短文中相关信息的关系，但存在以下一条或者多条问题： • 虽然整体上是根据题目的要求在写作，但仅能传达听力讲座与阅读短文之间某种含糊、笼统、不清晰、不太精确的关系； • 可能会漏掉听力讲座中一条要点； • 听力讲座或者阅读短文中的某些要点，或两者之间的关系表达得不完整、不准确； • 存在更多常见的语言错误，出现明显的、含糊的表达方式，传达语义、信息连贯方面模糊不清。
2	包含一些听力讲座中的相关信息，但是在表达听力讲座的信息或与阅读短文中相关信息的关系时，语言表达存在很大困难，遗漏大量信息或表达要点十分不准确，存在以下一条或者多条问题： • 严重歪曲或者完全遗漏了听力讲座与阅读短文之间的关系； • 严重歪曲或者遗漏了听力讲座中的要点； • 语言错误，关键地方的语义模糊、费解或不连贯。
1	存在以下一条或者多条问题： • 提供的内容很少，没有意义或与听力讲座的内容不相关； • 语言水平太低，无法理解。
0	仅能从阅读材料中抄袭句子，内容与主题无关，不用英语写作或交白卷。

15.4 独立写作评分标准（Scoring Criteria for Independent Writing）

表 15-3 独立写作评分标准

分数	任务描述
5	基本完成以下所有内容： • 有效地完成题目主题和任务； • 组织结构清晰，论证充分，能使用恰当和充分的解释、例证和细节； • 主题一致，衔接、过度有序，符合逻辑，语义连贯； • 语言前后使用一致，句式灵活，选词恰当、地道，可能有小的词汇和语法错误。
4	基本完成以下所有内容： • 很好地完成主题和任务，但某些要点可能没有充分阐述； • 组织结构清晰，论证充分，能使用恰当和充分的解释、例证和细节； • 主题一致，衔接、过度有序，符合逻辑，语义连贯，偶尔出现冗余、节外生枝，或不清楚的前后关系； • 语语言前后使用一致，句式灵活，选词恰当、地道，可能偶尔在结构上、词语形式或者用词的地道性方面出现明显的小错误，但不影响语义。
3	存在下面一条或者多条问题： • 使用不错的解释、例证和细节，基本完成主题和任务； • 主题一致，衔接、过度有序，基本符合逻辑，但语义偶尔费解； • 句法和词汇虽然准确，但是范围有限。
2	存在下面一条或者多条问题： • 有限地回应主题和任务； • 内容不完整，结构不清晰，信息不连贯； • 例证、解释、细节等论据不恰当、不充分； • 选词明显不恰当； • 大量的语言错误。
1	存在如下一条或者多条严重问题： • 组织结构混乱，内容无法展开； • 很少或根本没有细节，或不相关的细节，或对任务不相关的回应； • 大量严重的、常见的语言错误。
0	仅从题目中抄袭词汇，或内容与主题无关，不用英语写作或交白卷。

15.5 实战分析（Analysis of Writing Practice）

15.5.1 综合写作分析（Analysis of Integrated Writing）

综合写作试题以阅读和听力材料为基础，考生首先需要阅读一篇学术短文，然后听一段大约 2 分钟的讲座录音，在听录音时可以做笔记来帮助答题。考生共用 20 分钟的时间来总结听力讲座中的要点，并解释这些要点与阅读材料中要点的关系，并解释有何不同。在综合写作线上考试中，首先电脑屏幕左边会出现一段阅读材料，3 分钟后材料会自动消失，开始播放讲座录音。听力结束后，刚才隐去的阅读内容会在屏幕左边重新出现，考生在屏幕右侧的空白处输入作文。综合写作限时 20 分钟，字数要求是 150~225 字。

注意：

① 综合写作只要求考生解释听力讲座中的要点与阅读材料中的要点是如何相悖的，不允许考生发表个人观点；

② 考生如果只从阅读材料中抄袭词汇只能得 0 分；

③ 如果写作内容不谈及听力讲座，只涉及阅读材料，则仅得 1 分；

范例：

Writing Practice Set 3 (Integrated): Passage, Lecture, and Question

Directions: Give yourself 3 minutes to read the passage.

Reading Time: 3 minutes

　　Critics say that current voting systems used in the United States are inefficient and often lead to the inaccurate counting of votes. Miscounts can be especially damaging if an election is closely contested. Those critics would like the traditional systems to be replaced with far more efficient and trustworthy computerized voting systems.

　　In traditional voting, one major source of inaccuracy is that people accidentally vote for the wrong candidate. Voters usually have to find the name of their candidate on a large sheet of paper containing many names—the ballot—and make a small mark next to that name. People with poor eyesight can easily mark the wrong name. The computerized voting machines have an easy-to-use touch-screen technology: to cast a vote, a voter needs only to touch the candidate's name on the screen to record a vote for that candidate; voters can even have the computer magnify the name for easier viewing.

　　Another major problem with old voting systems is that they rely heavily on people to count the votes. Officials must often count up the votes one by one, going through every ballot and recording the vote. Since they have to deal with thousands of ballots, it is almost inevitable that they will make mistakes. If an error is detected, a long and expensive recount has to take place. In contrast, computerized systems remove the possibility of human error, since all the vote

counting is done quickly and automatically by the computers.

Finally, some people say it is too risky to implement complicated voting technology nationwide. But without giving it a thought, governments and individuals alike trust other complex computer technology every day to be perfectly accurate in banking transactions as well as in the communication of highly sensitive information.

听力讲座：

Directions: Here is the transcript.

Narrator: Now listen to part of a lecture on the topic you just read about.

Professor: While traditional voting systems have some problems, it's doubtful that computerized voting will make the situation any better. Computerized voting may seem easy for people who are used to computers. But what about people who aren't? People who can't afford computers, people who don't use them on a regular basis—these people will have trouble using computerized voting machines. These voters can easily cast the wrong vote or be discouraged from voting altogether because of fear of technology. Furthermore, it's true that humans make mistakes when they count up ballots by hand. But are we sure that computers will do a better job? After all, computers are programmed by humans, so "human error" can show up in mistakes in their programs. And the errors caused by these defective programs may be far more serious. The worst a human official can do is miss a few ballots. But an error in a computer program can result in thousands of votes being miscounted or even permanently removed from the record. And in many voting systems, there is no physical record of the votes, so a computer recount in the case of a suspected error is impossible! As for our trust of computer technology for banking and communications, remember one thing: these systems are used daily and they are used heavily. They didn't work flawlessly when they were first introduced. They had to be improved on until they got as reliable as they are today. But voting happens only once every two years nationally in the United States and not much more than twice a year in many local areas. This is hardly sufficient for us to develop confidence that computerized voting can be fully trusted.

Directions: Give yourself 20 minutes to plan and write your response. Your response is judged on the quality of the writing and on how well it presents the points in the lecture and

Part 4 Writing for Tests

their relationship to the reading passage. Typically, an effective response will be 150 to 225 words. You may view the reading passage while you respond.

Response time: 20 minutes

Question: Summarize the points made in the lecture, being sure to explain how they cast doubt on specific points made in the reading passage.

范文分析：

Writing Practice Set 3 (Integrated): Sample Responses Score of 5

The lecture（开头段：听力讲座的中心观点与阅读材料的中心观点是相悖的）explained why the computerized voting system can not replace the traditional voting system. There are the following three reasons（过渡句引出下文三条要点，即听力讲座和阅读短文三个分论点——对应的关系）.

First of all, not every one can use computers correctly（转述听力讲座的第一个分论点）. Some people do not have access to computers, some people are not used of computers, and some people are even scared of this new technology. If the voters do not know how to use a computer, how do you expect them to finish the voting process through computers?（转述听力讲座第一个分论点的细节支撑）This directly refutes the reading passage which states that computerized voting is easier by just touching the screen（指出听力讲座反驳阅读材料的第一个分论点）.

Secondly, computers may make mistakes as the people do（转述听力讲座第二个分论点）. As computers are programmed by the human beings, thus errors are inevitable in the computer system. Problems caused by computer voting systems may be more serious than those caused by people. A larger number of votes might be miss counted or even removed from the system. Furthermore, it would take more energy to recount the votes（转述听力讲座第二个分论点的细节支撑）. Again this contradicts what is stated in the reading which stated that only people will make mistakes in counting（指出听力讲座反驳阅读材料的第二个分论点）.

Thirdly, computerized voting system is not reliable because it has not reached a stable status（转述听力讲座的第三个分论点）. People trust computers to conduct banking transactions because the computerized banking system is being used daily and frequently and has been stable. However, the voting does not happen as often as banking thus the computerized

voting system has not been proved to be totally reliable（转述听力讲座第三个分论点的细节支撑，指出听力讲座反驳阅读材料的第三个分论点）.

All in all, not everyoen can use a computer properly, computer cause mistakes and computerized voting system is not reliable are the main reasons why computerized voting system can not replace the traditional voting system.（可以省略总结段，只要按照阅读材料的结构写四段即可：总—分—分—分结构。）

Score explanation 优点：

This response is well organized, selects the important information from all three points made in the lecture, and explains its relationship to the claims made in the reading passage about the advantages of computerized voting over traditional voting methods.

First, it counters the argument that computerized voting is more user-friendly and prevents distortion of the vote by saying that many voters find computers unfamiliar and some voters may end up not voting at all.

Second, it challenges the argument that computerized voting will result in fewer miscounts by pointing out that programming errors may result in large-scale miscounts and that some errors may result in the loss of voting records.

Third, it rejects the comparison of computerized voting with computerized banking by pointing out that the reliability of computerized banking ("reached a stable status") has been achieved though frequent use, which does not apply to voting.

瑕疵：

There are occasional minor language errors: for example, "people not used of computers" "miss counted" "computer cause mistakes", and the poor syntax of the last sentence ("All in all ..."). Some spelling errors are obviously typos: "everyoen". The errors, however, are not at all frequent and do not result in unclear or inaccurate representation of the content.

The response meets all the criteria for the score of 5.

写作步骤总结：

托福综合写作的阅读短文共四段，组织结构清晰，一般是总（中心论点）—分（分论点一）—分（分论点二）—分（分论点三）。听力讲座的内容结构与阅读材料一样，一般从中心论点到三个分论点逐一进行反驳和论证，掌握好这种对应关系就不会丢分。首先，阅读短文材料时按照顺序找出中心论点和三个分论点；然后，在听讲座时，记录反驳和论据中信息含量大、能帮助回忆起相关内容的关键词即可；最后，对照听力笔记和阅读短文，按照总—分—分—分的结构解释说明听力中的重要论据是如何反驳阅读短文的观点的。写完后可以按照表 15-2 评分标准中的 5 分和 4 分标准，对照检查和修改。

记住几个表达观点的关键词（见表 15-4）：

表 15-4 关键词表

赞同	agree with、approve、confirm、be convinced、support
反对	contradict、refute、challenge、oppose、reject、disapprove、disagree with
提出	Suggest、recommend、propose、mention
认为	argue、believe、claim、state、assert
证实	prove、clarify、illustrate、explain

15.5.2 独立写作分析：(Analysis of Independent Writing)

独立写作要求考生根据自己的知识和经验陈述、解释并支持对某一争议性问题或者观点的某种看法。本题在综合写作之后进行，线上考试时电脑界面左侧显示论述题目，右侧空格用来输入内容。独立写作限时 30 分钟，要求最少 300 字。

Direction: Read the question below. You have 30 minutes to plan, write and revise your essay. Typically, an effective response will contain a minimum of 300 words.

Question: Do you agree or disagree with the following statement? technology designed to make our life simpler, but actually makes our life more complicated.

Use specific reasons and examples to support your answer.

写作步骤分析：审题—立意—提纲—初稿—修改

审题：题目一般是有争议性的论点，主要考查考生的思辨能力。

立意：典型的独立写作结构是五段式作文。首先确立自己的立场，反对或支持都可以。确定立场后，用提纲确定文章的中心论点和两到三个分论点（三个最佳），然后用分析、解释、例子、细节等方式支撑分论点，最后得出结论，重申论点，深化和拓展主题。评分人员主要看理据、例子、细节的论述是否充分和恰当，是否有力地支撑了论点，篇章结构和脉络是否清晰，句子和词汇使用是否准确、得体、地道。

范文分析:

We have witnessed the remarkable advancements that technology has brought to our world. From the microwave oven to intercontinental guided missiles, computerized tomography (CT) to nanorobots, no one can deny the fact that technology has played and will play an essential role in the progress of mankind（开头段，列举事实并承认对方观点的合理性）. However, we are also confronted with the unprecedented problems caused by advanced technology（表明自己的立场）. I believe that technological progresses in the internet, transportation, and nuclear energy have resulted in our lives becoming much more complex than before（陈述中心论点并给出下文三个分论点的论述方向）.

To begin with, the internet is not always the kind-hearted and faithful helper that we believe it to be（第一个分论点，主体部分第一段的主题句）. The advent of internet has opened up a whole new world to humanity and many people feel that they have never been this close to other humans in a global sense（承认网络的好处，显得不偏激）. However, certain elements have been going astray from this idealized vision of the internet during past few years（重点是证明其坏处以支撑自己的论点）. Computer viruses are spread largely through the internet. Also, illegal business, such as unlicensed gambling and lotteries are breeding like flies, not to mention internet fraud which claims thousands of victims each year. What is worse, pornographic and violent videos, films and pictures are accessible to children despite repeated prohibition（列举事实，证明网络让人类生活更复杂）.

What is more, the introduction of new technology into transportation has caused fresh anxieties（第二个分论点，主体部分第二段的主题句）. Now, we are so accustomed to our needs being served almost immediately by technology that we find it frustrating to have something out of human control. This point is especially obvious in transportation. So dependent are we on high-tech means of transportation that any pitfall or small trouble with them considerably influences our travel plans. For example, cruise ships may be delayed by storms, flights may be canceled because of bad weather, and high-speed express trains, such as Euros-tar, maybe stuck in the freezing cold tunnel and lose power. Imagine how upset travelers get when they hear that their trip is delayed and they have to wait for another ten hours before

---

1 白瑜，高文成. 2018. 托福满分范文129篇精讲. 杭州：浙江教育出版社.

they can go aboard (论证快捷的交通工具会使人们变得沮丧和焦虑).

Traffic jams are another complication that was not an issue previous to the technological era (第二个让生活复杂化的例子). In big cities such as New York, Tokyo, Bangkok, and Beijing, the drivers complain about the endless traffic congestion that takes place on their roads every day. Time is wasted sitting in cars on the expressways, while so much poisonous gas is emitted into the atmosphere. People have to put up with these negative experiences that they never would have had to deal with before.

Moreover, nuclear energy leads our world to an uncertain ending which may be beyond most people's control (第三个分论点，也是主体段第三段的主题句). Nuclear energy was once considered the greatest invention mankind had seen, creating massive amounts of energy, and was used as an invincible force in World War II (承认核能源的好处). However, in retrospect, we must admit that it also generates terror and uncertainty (证明其坏处以支撑自己的论点). Take the nuclear leakage in Japan as another example. On March 11, a magnitude 9.0 earthquake devastated the north-east of the country and triggered a crisis at the Fukushima nuclear plant. All the residents had to be evacuated and the effect that the leakage may have on their health is uncertain. This incident is a painful reminder of the notorious Chernobyl disaster. It has yet to be decided whether this unconquered power is a blessing or a curse (以日本核泄漏为例，证明核科技带给人类的危害，使生活复杂化).

To sum up, while technology does improve the living conditions of humans and civilizations on earth, it also gives rise to many complications (结尾段重申观点，但未深化或拓展主题，稍有欠缺).

写作实践 Writing Tasks

▶▶ 综合写作：(Integrated Writing)

Directions: Give yourself 3 minutes to read the passage.

Reading Time: 3 minutes

Reading passage

In the United States, it had been common practice since the late 1960s not to suppress natural forest fires. The "let it burn" policy assumed that forest fires would burn themselves out quickly, without causing much damage. However, in the summer of 1988, forest fires in Yellowstone, the most famous national park in the country, burned for more than two months and spread over a huge area, encompassing more than 800, 000 acres. Because of the large-scale damage, many people called for replacing the "let it burn" policy with a policy of extinguishing forest fires as soon as they appeared. Three kinds of damage caused by the "let it burn" policy were emphasized by critics of the policy.

First, Yellowstone fires caused tremendous damage to the park's trees and other vegetation. When the fires finally died out, nearly one third of Yellowstone's land had been scorched. Trees were charred and blackened from flames and smoke. Smaller plants were entirely incinerated. What had been a national treasure now seemed like a devastated wasteland.

Second, the park wildlife was affected as well. Large animals like deer and elk were seen fleeing the fire. Many smaller species were probably unable to escape. There was also concern that the destruction of habitats and the disruption of food chains would make it impossible for the animals that survived the fire to return.

Third, the fires compromised the value of the park as a tourist attraction, which in turn had negative consequences for the local economy. With several thousand acres of the park engulfed in flames, the tourist season was cut short, and a large number of visitors decided to stay away. Of course, local businesses that depended on park visitors suffered as a result.

Directions: Here is the transcript of lecture.

Actually, fires are a natural part of the ecological cycle and their role is not just destructive but also creative. That is why the "let it burn" policy is fundamentally a good one, even if it sometimes causes fires like the 1988 Yellowstone fire. Let's look at what happened after the 1988 Yellowstone fire.

First, vegetation. As you might imagine, scorched areas were in time were colonized by new plants. As a matter of fact, the plants in Yellowstone became more diverse because the fire created an opportunity for certain plants that could not grow otherwise. For example, areas where the trees have been destroyed by fire could now be taken over by smaller plants that needed open and shaded space to grow. In another example, seeds of certain plants species won't germinate unless they're exposed to very high levels of heat. Those plants started appearing alter the fire as well.

It's a similar story with the animals. Not only did their population recover, but the fire also created new opportunities. For instance, the small plants that replaced trees after the fire created an ideal habitat for certain small animals like rabbits and hares. When rabbits and hares started thriving, so did some predators that depended on them for food. So, certain food chains actually became stronger after the fire than before.

And last, fires like the 1988 Yellowstone fire would be a problem tor tourism if they happened every year. But they don't. It was a very unusual combination of factors that year, low rainfall, unusually strong winds, accumulation of dry undergrowth that caused the fire to be so massive. This combination has not occurred since and Yellowstone has not seen such a fire since 1988. Visitors came back to the park next year and each year after that.

Directions: Give yourself 20 minutes to plan and write your response. Your response is judged on the quality of the writing and on how well it presents the points in the lecture and their relationship to the reading passage. Typically, an effective response will be 150 to 225 words. You may view the reading passage while you respond.

Response time: 20 minutes

Question: Summarize the points made in the lecture, being sure to explain how they cast doubt on specific points made in the reading passage.

▶▶ 独立写作：(Independent Writing)

Directions: Read the question below. You have 30 minutes to plan, write and revise your essay. Typically, an effective response will contain a minimum of 300 words.

Question:

Do you agree or disagree with the following statement? Face-to-face communication is better than other types of communication, such as letters, email, or telephone calls.

Use specific reasons and details to support your answer.

第 16 单元 考研英语写作
Unit 16 Writing for National Postgraduate Entrance Examination

学习目标 Learning Objectives

1. 了解研究生入学英语考试作文的评分标准和原则；
2. 掌握研究生入学英语考试作文的写作步骤。

课前任务 Pretask

请给下面考试题目写出文章提纲。

Directions[1]: Write an essay of 160~200 words based on the following drawing. In your essay, you should:

① describe the drawing briefly,

② interpret its intended meaning, and

③ give your comments.

图 16-1 手机时代的聚会

1　何钢，印建坤．2019.2020 考研英语（一）写作范文 100 篇．北京：群言出版社．

引言 Introduction

从 2010 年起，我国研究生入学英语考试形式分为两种：其中**英语（一）**主要针对学术型硕士申请者；**英语（二）**主要针对专业硕士申请者。英语（一）写作部分共 30 分，占卷面总分值 30%；而英语（二）写作部分共 25 分，占卷面总分值 25%。英语（一）和英语（二）的写作部分都由两篇作文构成，分别是应用文写作和短文写作。应用文写作主要是各类书信、通知、备忘录等，考查的是考生基本的书信沟通能力；短文部分，英语（一）历年的真题主要考查的是看图书说话型作文，而英语（二）主要是图表式作文（见表 16-1）：

表 16-1 考查内容

类别	节	提供的信息	语言	题型	题目数量	计分
英语（一）写作 30 分	A	规定情境	英语	应用文（约 100 词）	1	10
	B	主题词、写作提纲、规定情境、图画、图表、图片等	英语	短文写作（160~200 词）	1	20
英语（二）写作 25 分	A	规定情境	英语	应用文（约 100 词）	1	10
	B	规定情境、提纲、图表等	英语	短文写作（约 150 词）	1	15

知识要点 Key Knowledge

16.1 评分原则（Scoring Principles）

① A 节应用文的评分侧重点在于信息点的覆盖和内容的组织、语言的准确性、格式和语域的恰当，对语法结构和词汇多样性的要求将根据具体试题做调整。作文中允许使用提示语中出现的关键词，但使用提示语中出现过的词组或句子将被扣分。B 节作文的评分重点在于内容的完整性、文章的组织连贯性、语法结构和词汇的多样性及语言的准确性。

② 评分人员先根据文章的内容和语言确定其所属档次，然后以该档次的要求来给分。每档有 1~3 分的调节分。

③ A 节作文的字数要求是 100 词左右。英语（一）B 节作文的字数要求是 160~200 词，英语（二）B 节作文的字数要求是 150 词。文章长度不符合要求的，酌情扣分。

④ 拼写与标点符号是语言准确性的一个方面。评分人员会视其对阅读理解的影响程度予以考虑评分，但英、美拼写及词汇用法均可接受。

⑤ 如书写较差，以致影响理解，会将分数降低一个档次。

16.2 评分标准（Scoring Criteria）

16.2.1 英语（一）评分标准（Scoring Criteria for English I）

第五档：A 节（9~10 分），B 节（17~20 分）

很好地完成了试题规定的任务：

- 包含所有内容要点；
- 使用丰富的语法结构和词汇；
- 语言自然流畅，语法错误极少；
- 有效地采用了多种衔接手法，文字连贯，层次清晰；
- 格式和语域恰当贴切。

第四档：A 节（7~8 分），B 节（13~16 分）

较好地完成了试题规定的任务：

- 包含所有内容要点，漏掉一两个次重点；
- 使用较丰富的语法结构和词汇；
- 语言基本准确，只有在使用较复杂结构或较高级词汇时才有个别语法错误；
- 采用了适当的衔接手法，层次清晰，组织较严密；
- 格式和语域较恰当。

第三档：A 节（5~6 分），B 节（9~12 分）

基本完成了试题规定的任务：

- 虽漏掉一些内容，但包含多数内容要点；
- 语法结构和词汇能满足任务的需求；
- 有一些语法及词汇错误，但不影响理解；
- 采用了简单的衔接手法，内容较连贯，层次较清晰；
- 格式和语域基本合理。

第二档：A 节（3~4 分），B 节（5~8 分）

未能按要求完成题目规定的任务，未能清楚地传达信息给读者：

- 漏掉或未能有效阐述要点，写了一些无关内容；
- 语法结构单调、词汇量有限；
- 有较多语法结构及词汇方面的错误，影响理解；
- 未采用恰当的衔接手法，内容缺少连贯性；
- 格式和语域不恰当。

第一档：A节（1~2分），B节（1~4分）
未完成题目规定的任务，未能传达信息给读者：

- 遗漏主要信息，且有许多不相关的内容；
- 语法和词汇使用单调、重复；
- 语言错误多，语言运用能力差；
- 未采用任何衔接手法，内容不连贯，缺少组织和分段；
- 无格式和语域概念。

零档（0分）
所传达的信息太少，内容与要求无关或无法辨认，无法评价。

16.2.2 英语（二）评分标准（Scoring Criteria for English II）

第五档：A节（9~10分），B节（13~15分）
很好地完成了试题规定的任务：

- 包含所有内容要点；
- 使用丰富的语法结构和词汇；
- 语言自然流畅，基本上没有语法错误；
- 有效地采用了多种衔接手法，文字连贯，层次清晰；
- 格式和语域恰当贴切。

第四档：A节（7~8分），B节（10~12分）
较好地完成了题目规定的任务：

- 包含所有内容要点，允许漏掉一两个次重点；
- 使用较丰富的语法结构和词汇；
- 语言基本准确，只有在使用较复杂结构或较高级词汇时才有个别语法错误；

- 采用了适当的衔接手法，层次清晰，组织较严密；
- 格式和语域较恰当。

第三档：A 节（5~6 分），B 节（7~9 分）
基本完成了题目规定的任务：

- 虽漏掉一些内容，但包含多数内容要点；
- 语法结构和词汇能满足要求；
- 存在一些语法及词汇错误，但不影响整体理解；
- 采用了简单的衔接手法，内容基本连贯，层次基本清晰；
- 格式和语域基本合理。

第二档：A 节（3~4 分），B 节（4~6 分）
未能按要求完成题目规定的任务：

- 漏掉或未能有效阐述一些内容要点，写了一些无关内容；
- 语法结构单调、词汇使用有限；
- 存在较多语法结构及词汇方面的错误，影响理解；
- 未采用恰当的衔接手法，内容缺少连贯性；
- 格式和语域不恰当。

第一档：A 节（1~2 分），B 节（1~3 分）
未完成题目规定的任务：

- 明显遗漏主要内容，且有许多不相关的内容；
- 语法结构和词汇的使用单调、重复；
- 语言错误多，有碍读者对内容的理解，语言运用能力差；
- 未采用任何衔接手法，内容不连贯，缺少组织和分段；
- 无格式和语域概念。

零档（0 分）
所传达的信息或所使用语言太少，内容与要求无关或无法辨认，无法评价。

英语（一）和英语（二）都使用五档评分标准，具体内容基本相似。但是从各档表述词的差异上看，英语（二）的评价标准相对宽松一点。

16.3 实战分析（Analysis of Writing Practice）

16.3.1 英语（一）短文写作（Essay Writing for English Ⅰ）

英语（一）短文写作近年来主要考查漫画类作文，揭示的是社会热点问题和现象。下面以实例分析英语（一）的写作步骤：审题—立意—提纲—初稿—修改。

Directions[1]: Write an essay of 160~200 words based on the following drawing. In your essay, you should:

① describe the drawing briefly,

② interpret its intended meaning, and

③ give your comments.

图 16-2 旅程之"余"

审题：按照指令要求首先解读漫画（见表 16-2）：

表 16-2 审题内容

描述漫画	从时空两轴入手描述漫画内容：时间、地点、人物、事件、结果：湖中有一条小船，船上坐着一对游客，边吃零食，边游览。

立意：

① 按照指令第二条要求解释漫画的用意，根据漫画所暗示的含义从原因、结果、影响等角度分析、论证其含义，选择一个角度分析即可，由于篇幅所限，一般列出两到三条原因或结果即为充分的论证。

② 按照指令第三条要求对漫画揭示的问题或现象进行评价，考生应表达自己的立场、观点、是非或价值判断，观点要鲜明、有力。

③ 在结论段重申自己的观点和立场，同时可以展望未来或者给出解决问题的方案、建议，结束全文。

---

1 恋练团队 . 2018. 考研英语一写作宝典 . 北京：群言出版社 .

范文分析：

In the picture we see a boat sits a young couple who are eating snacks and casting the packaging into the lake filled with refuse（描述漫画内容）. The picture illustrates the phenomenon of environmental threat to scenic spots（指出漫画含义）.

There are two major factors that account for the environmental damage of scenic spots（具体分析两个原因）. In recent years, the tourism industry has been developing quickly; most scenic areas now accommodate ten times as many tourists as they did decades ago. These travelers will produce a huge volume of waste. The second problem is that administrations have not kept pace with this booming industry, so the refuse left by tourists is more than that can be disposed of. Therefore, the environment is getting worse.

To solve this problem, the waste disposition systems in scenic spots must be upgraded while certain laws need to be enforced to deter those who are inclined to litter waste（提出解决方案）. I believe through these efforts we can have clean and beautiful places to visit in the near future（展望未来，结束全文）.

初稿完成后按照表 16-3 内容修改并定稿。

表 16-3　修改对照表

内容	• 是否按照题目要求正确理解并描述漫画内容、动态图表揭示的变化、静态图表表达的数据分布。 • 原因或者结果分析是否充分，是否符合现实和逻辑，是否针对漫画的含义发表个人观点和评价，是否针对动态图表中的变化或者趋势发表个人观点和评价，是否针对静态图表中的数据分布特点发表个人观点和评价，并论证和支撑自己的观点。 • 结论是否给人自然结束的感觉，是否预测未来或者提供建议。
结构	• 文章是否至少分开头、主体、结论三段，是否按照指令的提纲所写。 • 句子之间的衔接、过渡是否自然和符合逻辑，是否使用过渡和衔接的词汇。
语言	• 用词是否准确、恰当、生动、具体、地道，句子是否简洁、完整、充分地表达了语义，句式是否富有变化，符合修辞和语法规则。 • 是否有以下常见用词错误：拼写错误、单复数错误、a/the 的滥用或者省略、动词的时态错误、词语搭配错误、代词的指示错误、人称前后不一致、生僻词、俚语或口语化的表达方式、陈旧的表达方式、啰唆的表达方式、故作高深的表达方式。 • 是否有以下常见句子错误：语义前后矛盾或者违背常识和逻辑、句子结构前后不平行、主谓不一致、粘连句、主从句倒置、句式杂糅、修饰语悬垂、句子结构残缺等。

16.3.2　英语（二）短文写作（Essay Writing for English Ⅱ）

英语（二）短文写作近年来考察的图表题主要分两种：动态图表和静态图表，其中动态图表主要体现一定时间周期内某个事物或者现象的变化和趋势；而静态图表主要是涉及某个主题相关数据的静态分布。下面以实例分析英语（二）的写作步骤：审题 — 立意 — 提纲 — 初稿 — 修改。

例题 1

Directions[1]: Write an essay based on the chart below. In your writing, you should:

① interpret the chart, and

② give your comments.

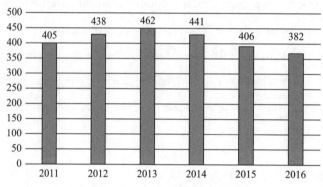

图 16-3　中国方便面销售情况（亿元）

审题：按照指令要求首先解读图表内涵（见表 16-4）：

表 16-4　审题内容

图表类型	动态图
图表内容	• 整体描述：2011—2016 年我国方便面销售情况的变化。 • 具体变化：2011—2013 年方便面销量逐年上升，2013 方便面销售达到峰值后，2014—2016 年呈现逐年下降的趋势。

立意：

按照指令要求第二步针对图表内涵进行分析评价，动态图一般是分析变化或者形成趋势的原因，能找出两到三个原因解释变化即可。但也有的题目可能需要分析结果或者影响，一般分析两到三条结果或者影响即为充分的分析。

原因一：国人生活质量提高，意识到方便面是垃圾食品。

1　恋练团队 . 2018. 考研英语二写作宝典 . 北京：群言出版社 .

原因二：方便面的消费主力——返乡人员。

原因三：外卖的普及对方便面的替代。

由于写作的指令是提纲式的，所以审题立意后可以省略提纲这一步。

范文分析：

> The bar chart illustrates the change of instant noodle market in China from 2011 to 2016 (按照要求开头段要整体描述图表). Over the period, while the sales of instant noodles rose steadily to a record high of more than 46 billion yuan in 2013, they started to decline markedly from 2014. By 2016, the sales have shrunk to around 38 billion yuan (具体描述图表暗示的变化).
>
> There are several reasons behind this market shrinking (主体段落分析三个原因). First, due to the raised awareness of food and health, many Chinese people have started to reject instant noodles as unhealthy foods. Second, instant noodles are most favored by rural migrant workers as a kind of cheap and tasty staple food. But with more and more migrant workers returning to their hometowns, instant noodles have also lost a large portion of its market. Finally, the dramatic popularization of food delivery service largely weakened the key advantage of instant noodles—convenience.
>
> Judging from the current situation, we may predict that the sales of instant noodles will further decline (结论段首先预测未来趋势). To regain their market, noodles manufacturers will have to make great efforts in upgrading the product lines, launching new and unique flavors, redesigning product packaging, while considering seriously about how to turn instant noodles into healthier foods (提出具体建议，结束全文).

初稿完成后按照表 16-3 内容修改并定稿。

例题 2

Directions[1]: Write an essay based on the chart below. In your writing, you should:

① interpret the chart, and

② give your comments.

---

[1] 恋练团队. 2018. 考研英语二写作宝典. 北京：群言出版社.

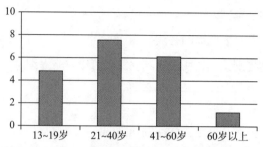

图 16-4 某小区不同年龄段居民日均上网时间（小时）

审题：按照指令要求首先解读图表内涵（见表 16-5）：

表 16-5 审题内容

图表类型	静态图
图表内容	• 整体描述：图表揭示某小区不同年龄段居民日均上网时间。 • 具体数据分布特点：21~40 岁人群上网时长最长，60 岁以上人群上网时长最短。13~19 岁和 41~60 岁人群上网时长适中。

立意：

按照指令要求第二步针对图表内涵进行分析评价，静态图一般是分析数据分布的特点以及成因，并表达自己的看法，最后给出合理的建议。由于写作的指令是提纲式的，所以审题立意后可以省略提纲这一步。

范文分析：

  The bar chart shows the time people of different age groups in a community spend on the Internet per day（整体描述）. To be specific, teenagers spend around 5 hours per day on the Internet, while the figure for people between 21 and 40 is almost 8 hours. The 41-to-60-year-olds and the over-60s surf the Internet for about 6 hours and 1 hour each day, respectively（具体数据分布特点描述）.

  The amount of time spent on the internet varies among different groups due to their purposes. Teenagers use the Internet mainly to communicate with their peers via instant messaging apps and to focus on discussing the latest news. The middle-aged need Internet access to deal with their work or business or to make various kinds of investments. Senior citizens may browse websites for health-care information or local news（分析上网目的的不同）.

  Although the Internet largely satisfies different needs, it also presents risks that might end up reducing one's quality of life（表达观点）. For example, surfing online means sitting in front of a computer or staring at a cell-phone screen for extended periods of time. As a result, people might suffer from eye conditions, headache, or neck problems (支撑观点). It is better to take regular breaks when spending a whole day online (提出建议).

写作实践 Writing Tasks

英语（一）(English I)

漫画

Directions: Write an essay of 160~200 words based on the following drawing. In your essay, you should:

① describe the drawing briefly,

② interpret its intended meaning, and

③ give your comments.

图 16-5　手机时代的聚会

英语（二）(English II)

（1）静态图表

Directions: Write an essay based on the chart below. In your writing, you should:

① interpret the chart, and

② give your comments.

表 16-6　2018 级本科生和研究生毕业去向

毕业去向	总体情况		本科生		研究生	
	人数	比例	人数	比例	人数	比例
国内升学	2,292	26.73%	2,243	46.24%	49	1.32%
出国（境）深造	1,054	12.29%	1,004	20.70%	50	1.34%

续表

毕业去向	总体情况		本科生		研究生	
	人数	比例	人数	比例	人数	比例
单位就业	4,967	57.92%	1,437	29.62%	3,530	94.79%
自主创业	10	0.12%	3	0.06%	7	0.19%
未就业	252	2.94%	164	3.38%	88	2.36%
合计	8,575	100%	4,851	100%	3,724	100%

（2）动态图表

Directions: Write an essay based on the chart below. In your writing, you should:

① interpret the chart, and

② give your comments.

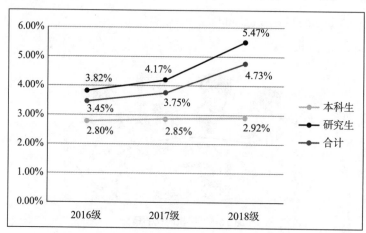

图 16-6　近三年毕业生到基层及艰苦边远地区就业情况

第五部分　写作与语法
Part 5　Writing and Grammar

内容提要
Preview

　　语法是英语写作的基础，本部分主要介绍基本语法，主要包括四个单元：词汇、句子、语法、标点。第 17 单元词汇部分介绍如何选择合理的措辞，第 18 单元句子介绍如何书写正确的英文句子；第 19 单元语法介绍如何避免一些常见的语法错误，第 20 单元标点介绍如何正确使用英语中的标点符号。

第 17 单元　词汇
Unit 17　Diction

学习目标 Learning Objectives

1. 了解词汇的合理使用；
2. 掌握词汇的四个"正确"。

课前任务 Pretask

仔细观察下面的句子，找出这些句子中词汇使用不合理的地方并修改。

- His grandfather kicked the bucket last night. We would like to give our condolences.
- I questioned him about the course I should take.
- The weather here is very bad.
- She received the first prize in the competition.

引言 Introduction

　　词汇是最小，也是最基本的写作单元。但写作中一般都会存在词汇使用错误的情况，有些不仅是用错词，而且词汇使用不合理、不规范或不地道。因此，本单元主要介绍如何合理地使用英语词汇。总体而言，须做到四个"正确"：正确的词语类别、正确的词语意义、正确的词语范围，以及正确的词语搭配。

知识要点 Key Knowledge

17.1　正确的词语类别（Correct Word Type）

　　正确的词语类别主要是从词语层级出发，将词汇分为标准词汇和非标准词汇两大类别。标准词汇可进一步分为：正式与专业词汇（formal and technical words）、非正式词汇（informal words）及普通词汇（common words）。

17.1.1　词语类别介绍（Word Type）

正式及专业词汇一般是较复杂、较长的"大词"及专业性较强的词汇，一般出现在正式的演讲文中，如学术讲座、科技文献、官方文件、商务信函和公共演讲等。非正式词汇主要出现在日常生活的对话中，语言比较随意，通常是较短、较简单的"小词"。但非正式词汇并非只能出现在口头交流中，生活信件、电子邮件、短信中同样也可以使用非正式词汇。请对比表17-1中的正式与非正式词汇：

表17-1　正式与非正式用语对比

非正式	正式
smart	highly developed intelligence
baby	infant
bad results	negative consequences
guys/ you guys	ladies and gentlemen

大多数英语词汇，既非正式词汇，也非非正式词汇，这些即为普通词汇。普通词汇可出现在日常生活及各种写作类型中，既易懂，又符合写作规范，是大学英语写作中使用最为广泛的词汇。请对比以下三个段落中的词语：

- It's a very bad idea for women with babies to drink wine. When they drink, the alcohol will go straight into their blood and will spread all over her body, including the baby.
- The negative effects of alcohol on the unborn child are very serious. When the expectant mother drinks, alcohol is absorbed into her bloodstream and distributed throughout her entire body.
- The deleterious effects of alcohol on the unborn child are very serious. When a pregnant woman consumes alcohol, the ethanol in the bloodstream easily crosses the placenta from mother to child and invades the amniotic fluid.

从这三句话可以看出，第一句用语较为随意，词语短小，词组较多，使用了如 bad、babies、go straight into、spread all over 等口语词汇，属于非正式用语；第二句话中大多为普通词汇，用语较为正式；第三句话中的词语较大，使用了如 deleterious、ethanol、bloodstream、placenta、amniotic fluid 等较专业的词汇，属于正式及专业用语。这三句话可用于不同场合和不同人群，其中第二句话的受众最为广泛，第一句更适用于非正式场合，而第三句则更适用于正式场合，或有一定专业知识背景的人群。

非标准词汇主要指俚语、行话、方言及生僻词等。这些词生动有趣，被各行各业的人们广泛使用，但通常不能用于正式写作。例如 His grandfather kicked the bucket last night. We would like to give our condolences. 这句话中的 kick the bucket 是英文俚语，义同中文的"翘辫子"。这明显不符合本句的语用场景，故用较为正式的 passed away 更合适。

17.1.2 正式用语的常见规则（Common Rules in Formal Word）

1）在正式用语中，如果可使用动词，则不使用动词词组。请对比表 17-2 中的词汇：

表 17-2 动词词组与动词对比

动词词组	动词
look at	consider
look into	investigate
put off	postpone
come across	encounter

2）名词词组通常比动词或动词词组更正式，请对比表 17-3 中的词汇：

表 17-3 名词词组与动词或动词词组对比

名词词组	动词或动词词组
make a contribution	contribute
on the basis of	based on
be of great concern	be concerned
give consideration to	consider

3）名词词组通常比形容词更正式，请对比表 17-4 中的词汇：

表 17-4 名词词组与形容词对比

名词词组	形容词
of great value	valuable
of great importance	important
on a daily basis	everyday

17.2 正确的词语意义（Correct Word Meaning）

语义可以分为两个方面：原义（denotative meaning）和涵义（connotative meaning）。原义是指词语本身的含义，即字典中给出的定义。有些词语只有原义，尤其是科技类词汇或术语；而涵义是指该词语所暗含的、带有某种感情色彩的意义。根据情感色彩，涵义又可分为三类：贬义（negative）、中性（neutral）、褒义（positive）。

例如：The host family has provided students a <u>home</u> away from <u>home</u>.

home 的原义是 the place where one lives，而涵义是 a place of warmth, comfort and affection。根据例句中讲话人想表达的含义，第一个 home 表达的是涵义，而第二个 home 表达的是的原义。

17.2.1 英式及美式英语（English and American English）

相同的词义在英式英语和美式英语中用词可能不同。写作中无论使用英式英语还是美式英语，都应保持前后一致。请对比表 17-5 中的词汇：

表 17-5　英式英语与美式英语对比

英式英语	美式英语
autumn	fall
lift	elevator
lorry	truck
cross	angry
flat	apartment

17.2.2 不同语义强度（Different Semantic Strength）

语义相近的词语在表达程度上会有所区别，请对比表 17-6 中的词汇语义：

表 17-6　词语强度对比

弱	强	更强
ask	question	interrogate
like	love	worship
big	large	huge

不同语义强度的词有时可根据程度进行替换，如：

- Beijing is a <u>big/large/huge</u> city.
- He did a(n) <u>good/great/excellent</u> job.

但有时不同语义强度的词也不可替换，如：

- He <u>asked</u> me about the course.（不可替换为 <u>questioned</u> 或 <u>interrogated</u>）
- They were <u>questioned</u> by the police.（表示质询，更正式，通常可问多个问题，可发生在任何场所）
- They were <u>interrogated</u> by the police.（表示审问，是官方形式，通常发生在审讯室）

17.2.3 不同感情色彩（Different Emotional Implications）

虽然不同词语的语义可能相近，但暗含的感情色彩可能不同。

例1：She is not a friend but a nodding acquaintance.

本句中"friend"比"acquaintance"表示了更为亲近的关系。

例2：I lived in a small town.

　　　I lived in a little town where I spent my happy childhood.

本句中 small 不含感情色彩，是对小镇的客观描述；而 little 暗含对小镇喜爱的感情色彩。

例3：*I work in the propaganda department of our school.

　　　I work in the marketing department of our school.

Propaganda 通常为贬义，指一个论述或观点的片面或不完整表述，经常用于宣传并有意识地影响他人的思想。因此，本句不应用 propoganda，而应用 marketing。

17.2.4 不同词语搭配（Different Word Collocations）

语义相近的词语在词语搭配上可能不同，同义词可以避免相同词汇的反复出现，更加丰富，语言更生动。例如，"think"可以用 argue、hold、contend、maintain、insist 或 consider 替换；"many"和"a lot of"可以用 numerous、countless、innumerable、a good deal of、a good/great many 等替换。请对比表 17-7 中的词语搭配：

表 17-7　词语搭配对比

语义	搭配
表示坚持	cling to insist on persist in
表示遵守	abide by adhere to comply with conform to
表示腐败、坏掉	rotten tomatoes addled eggs sour milk rancid butter

17.3 正确的词语范围（Correct Word Scope）

17.3.1 上下义关系（Hyponymy）

上下义关系是指两个词之间其中一个词的意义包含了另一个词的意义，是表示类概念（genus）的词项和表示种概念（species）词项的一种纵向关系。它们之间的语义关系即上下义关系，即上义词的意义包含了下义词的意义。上义词（superordinate）是对事物的概括性和抽象性说明；下义词（hyponym）是事物的具体表现形式或更为具体的说明（见表17-8）。

表17-8 上义词与下义词对比

上义词	下义词
flower	rose, lily, tulip, peony, carnation …
animal	lion, giraffe, zebra, monkey, fox, cat …
bird	parrot, robin, sparrow, cardinal, oriole …

下义词在写作中可以使描述更为具体。

例如：

She enjoys walking her dog and smell the flowers along the way.（上义词）

She enjoys walking her poodle and smell the roses along the way.（下义词）

注意：上下义关系不等同于整体与构件关系，如 human 和 arm、leg、head 等并不是上下义关系。

17.3.2 笼统与具体用词（General and Specific Words）

词语可以笼统（general），可以具体（specific）。写作初学者通常更倾向于使用较笼统的词汇。尽管笼统的词汇和具体的词汇在写作中都非常重要，但具体词汇可以使文章更生动、具体、清晰、令人印象深刻。

例如：He is a good man.

The food is good.

第一句中的"good"可以根据句义替换为 kind、honest、just、generous、sympathetic、warm-hearted、selfless、brave、honorable 等；第二句中的"good"可以根据句义替换为 tasty、delicious、nourishing、rich、wholesome、fresh、appetizing、abundant 等。

表17-9 笼统表达与具体表达

笼统	具体
living thing	animal, plant
animal	mammal, reptile, bird, fish

续表

笼统	具体
mammal	canine, feline, primate
canine	dog, fox, wolf
dog	poodle, golden retriever
It is very cold.	The biting cold pierce through my bones.
I travelled and it was great.	I flew to Beijing during the winter break and stayed there for three days. I visited the Summer Palace and enjoyed the Beijing roast duck.

一般来说，笼统词汇更加抽象，一般用于总结；具体词汇通常用于描述、解释或提供具体细节。写作时要灵活使用同义词、上下义词，使文章更生动有趣。

17.4　正确的词语搭配（Correct Word Collocation）

词语搭配是一个词语和另一个词语的前后组合。在英文中，很多词语有惯用或固定的词语搭配，不能任意组合。搭配错误也是写作中最常出现的错误之一，即便是同义词，词语搭配也可能完全不同。最常见的两种搭配问题为：动词搭配不当、形容词/副词搭配不当。

17.4.1　动词搭配不当（Improper Verb Collocation）

中文中很多词语的词义相同或相近，但在英文中却有不同的含义或搭配。例如，question 和 problem 在中文中都是"问题"，但在英文中的搭配不同。"solve the question"为不正确的搭配，应该是"answer the question"或"solve the problem"。再如，中文"得到"对应的英文单词是"receive"，因此可能会出现"receive the first prize"的搭配，但正确的搭配应该是"get/take/win the first prize"。类似的错误搭配还有：

- 错误：She catches up every chance to practice dancing.

  正确：She seizes/grasps/takes every chance to practice dancing.

- 错误：Our stomach can absorb the food.

  正确：Our stomach can digest the food.

- 错误：I have obtained two kilograms since the Spring Festival.

  正确：I have gained two kilograms since the Spring Festival.

- 错误：It is a good idea to study/learn knowledge through reading.

  正确：It is a good idea to acquire/gain/pursue knowledge through reading.

17.4.2　形容词/副词搭配不当（Improper Adjective/Adverbial Collocation）

受中文影响，写作时形容词或副词搭配不当也是常见问题之一。例如，学生常会说"I

understand deeply that …", 但更适当的搭配应该是 "I understand fully/thoroughly that …"。类似的错误搭配还有:

- 错误: This is considered one of her typical songs.
  正确: This is considered one of her representative songs.
- 错误: He is quite lively in class activities.
  正确: He is quite active in class activities.
- 错误: Those memories are expensive to me.
  正确: Those memories are precious to me.
- 错误: As an old customer of the supermarket, I did not complain.
  正确: As a regular customer of the supermarket, I did not complain.

在选词时,我们可以遵循以下原则:

- 通用写作中通常使用普通词;正式、专业和非标准用语一般只用于特殊场合和目的;
- 细节描述中使用具体词汇,小结或总结中使用笼统或抽象词汇;
- 在适当的场合使用习语表达,避免生搬硬套;
- 选择同义词时,选择最适合上下文和文体风格的词语。

写作实践 Writing Tasks

▶▶ Find the formal equivalents of the following common or informal words.

Common or informal words	Formal equivalents
deep	
about	
ask	
enough	
help	
buy	
wet	
put	

Part 5 Writing and Grammar

▶▶ **Rewrite the sentences in a more formal style using the verbs from the list below. Note that you may need to change the verb tense.**

A. raise B. assist C. increase D. conceal

E. participate F. reduce G. postpone

(1) We thought you'd been brought in from London to help out the local police.

(2) We encourage students to take part fully in the volunteer programs.

(3) He brought up a sensitive subject that everyone was trying to avoid.

(4) Costs have been cut down by 20% over the past year.

(5) He tried his best to cover up the truth.

(6) The game has already been put off three times.

(7) Expenditure on child education has gone up greatly over the past decade.

Take a quiz

第 18 单元　句子
Unit 18　Sentence

学习目标 Learning Objectives

1. 了解英文句子的特点；
2. 掌握英文句子的一致性、连贯性、简明性、多样性。

课前任务 Pretask

仔细观察下面的句子，判断这些句子是否正确、有效，并做必要的修改。

- Born in Xi'an, I became an engineer.
- I didn't sleep well last night, and my mom was ill.
- I studied in this university and this university was one of the best universities in the city.
- My mom is a science teacher. My dad is an engineer. They both love science. I also love science. My sister doesn't like science.

引言 Introduction

有了正确的用词，我们就可以搭建用来传达思想的句子和段落了。句子是段落的基础，好的文章最大的特点就是有正确、有效的句子。何为正确的句子？正确的句子应当：

- 有完整的结构；
- 有正确的语法和拼写；
- 首字母大写；
- 以句号、问号或感叹号结尾。

何为有效的句子？有效的句子应当：

- 前后一致，表达一个中心思想；
- 通顺、连贯、有逻辑性；

- 简单清晰；
- 结构多样，朗朗上口；
- 有重点。

知识要点 Key Knowledge

18.1 一致性（Unity）

一致性是有效句子的首要特点。一致性是指句子所表达的中心思想只有一个，并且是一个完整的统一体。但是只有一个中心思想并不代表句子都要简单、短小，长句也可做到思想统一。长句通常有一个中心思想，并由不同的附加思想或几个平行思想修饰或支撑。也就是说，紧密联系的意义可以在一个句子中表达，而不相关或关联不紧密的意义通常不可放在一个句子中。

例如：*Born in Beijing, he later became a famous actor.

本句虽然语法正确，但是前后两个部分并没有直接关联。Born in Beijing 并不能够直接带来 became a famous actor 这个结果。因此，本句缺乏一致性。若改写本句，则需加上一些可以让他成为著名演员的附加条件，如教育、工作背景等，以增强句子前后关联。

例如：Born in Beijing, he studied in Beijing Film Academy and later became a famous actor.

这种修改法使本句更具一致性。对缺乏一致性的句子一般有两种处理方法：

（1）删减句中与中心思想无关的内容。

范例：

- 不一致：Parking space in the downtown area, which is one of the most unsanitary part of the city, has become completely inadequate, but recently the city council voted to increase bus fares again.

- 一致：Parking space in the downtown area has become completely inadequate, but recently the city council voted to increase bus fares again.

（2）改写结构过于松散，未能清晰地表示中心思想的句子。

范例：

- 不一致：I got up early, and mom told me that there was always traffic jam.

- 一致：I got up early Monday morning because mom told me that there was always heavy traffic on Monday morning, so we'd better start earlier.

18.2 连贯性（Coherence）

连贯指句中的成分之间具有合乎逻辑的有机联系，思路清晰，意义相关，逻辑无误，语法规范，使听者或读者容易得到要领，不出现误解。"一致性"是指句中的成分都要围绕和服务于全句中心思想的表达，即与中心思想形成有机联系；"连贯性"则是指句中的成分之间要形成有机的横向联系。"一致性"和"连贯性"两者之间既有区别，又密切相关。

例如：*Everyone jumped up and cheered and the result was announced that China had won the gold medal. 这是一个并列句，其两个分句之间虽有 and 连接，但并未能表示出两个分句之间的逻辑联系，即未达到连贯要求，因而也未能实现句子的一致，整句的思想表达得不清楚。因此，本句应改为：

The result was announced that China had won the gold medal, and/so everyone jumped up and cheered.

或：As/When the result was announced that China had won the gold medal, everyone jumped up and cheered.

或：Everyone jumped up and cheered because/when the result was announced that China had won the gold medal.

从语法角度看，影响到句子连贯的因素主要包括：并列结构安排失当、代词所指对象不明确、垂悬修饰或修饰语错位、时态、人称、数或语气不一致，句子结构混乱等。要做到句子连贯，应遵循以下六个原则：

（1）除非必要，避免拆分紧密相连的词语，如：

不连贯：Look at that ridiculous lady's hat!

连贯：Look at that lady's ridiculous hat!

本句中 ridiculous 和 hat 紧密相连，如果拆分，ridiculous 修饰 lady，引发误解。

（2）避免使用指代不清的代词，如：

*She told her daughter that she had made the right choice.

本句中第二个 she 指代不明，不知道是指代讲话者还是她女儿，可改为：

She said to her daughter, "You have made the right choice."

或 She told her daughter that she herself had made the right choice.

再如：

- 不连贯：She skipped class to go to a lecture on interpreting skills, because he is a well-known interpreter.
- 连贯：She skipped class to go to a lecture on interpreting skills, because the speaker is a well-known interpreter.

（3）避免使用垂悬修饰语，或使修饰语与被修饰语距离过远，如：

*Looking out of the window, the smog is all we can see.

本句中 looking out 的施动者是人，而主句中的主语是 the smog，属于悬垂结构。应改为：Looking out of the window, we can see nothing but smog.

再如：

- 不连贯：Badly wounded, we sent the soldier to hospital.
- 连贯：Badly wounded, the soldier was sent to hospital.

（4）避免不必要的人称或数的变化，如：

*Those who want to join the math club should sign your name on this sheet of paper.

本句中 Those who 是第三人称复数，you（your）是第二人称，前后不一致，应改为：Those who want to join the math club should sign their names on this sheet of paper.

再如：

Every top official should go and spend several days in a number of impoverished villages before they make decisions concerning the alleviation of poverty.

本句中代词 they 与所指代的"Every top officials"单复数不一致，可以改为：

All top officials should go and spend several days in a number of impoverished villages before they make decisions concerning the alleviation of poverty.

（5）避免不必要的动词语态、时态、情态变化，如：

*The bomb destroyed the entire building and several people were injured in the bombing.

本句中前句使用主动语态 destroyed，后句使用被动语态 were injured，句子冗长不连贯，可以改为：

The bomb destroyed the entire building and injured several people.

（6）避免使用不同结构来表达平行结构，如：

*It is generally believed that one's action is more important than what one says.

此处平行结构使用了 one's action 和 what one says 两种不同表达，应改为：

It is generally believed that one's action is more important than one's words.

从修辞角度看，词语选用不当、辞格应用不当、重复、省略等其他修辞手法运用不当，都会影响到句子的连贯性（同时也会破坏句子的一致性）。

18.3 简明性（Conciseness）

简明性是指句子简单明了，没有多余成分。英语强调通过简洁而非复杂的语言进行交流，以有效交流和理解为目标。通常情况下，少就是多。要使句子简明，应当去掉非必要词语、非必要重复及无意义成分。

例如：

In the month of March, I started to check up on the Internet for the universities I might apply to. When I finished checking up, I made a list of these universities. After making the list, I tried to find as much information about these universities as possible. According to the information I found, one of these universities was located in a city by the sea. This university has a beautiful campus. From the campus, one can have a good view of the blue sea. I love the color blue.

本段文字开头的 In the month of March 中的 the month of 是非必要词汇，可以删除，不影响本意；段落最后 I love the color blue 与本段文字描述内容关系不紧密，是无意义成分，可以删除。除此之外，本段文字还出现了大量重复词汇，universities 出现了 5 次，check up、information、campus、sea 等都重复出现，语言繁琐冗长。本句可以修改为：

In March, I started to research on the Internet for the universities I might apply to. After making a list of them, I tried to find as much information as possible. One of them I found was located in a coastal city. It has a beautiful campus, from which one can have a good view of the blue sea.

除了去掉非必要词语、非必要重复及无意义成分，要做到句子简明，还应遵循以下规则：

（1）若句子主语清晰，可用代词替代重复出现的名词。

如前例中的"According to the information I found, one of these universities was located in a city by the sea. This university has a beautiful campus."主语清晰，可用 It 替换 This university。

（2）能使用一个词时则不使用短语，能使用短语时则不使用从句。

如前例中的"I started to check up on the Internet for the universities I might apply to"，check up 可以更换为 research。

（3）避免在本句或邻近句中使用重复词汇，除非为了凸出强调。

如前例中的 universities 在修改后可替换为 them，或省略。

（4）避免在同句中重复使用同义词语。

例如：

- 冗长：In May, people of different professions from all walks of life will gather for the celebration.
- 简洁：In May, people from all walks of life will gather for the celebration.

（5）句首避免过度使用 it + be-verb 或 there + be-verb 结构。

例如：There are three questions that should be answered.（冗长）

- Three questions should be answered.（简洁）

（6）避免使用过多被动语态。

英文倾向于使用被动语态。被动语态常以物、抽象概念或形式主语做主语，可以增强句子的客观性，因此经常出现在正式文书中。

例如：

It has been noted with concern that the stock of books in the library has been declining alarmingly. Students are asked to remind themselves of the rules for the borrowing and return of books, and to bear in mind the needs of other students. Penalties for overdue books will in the future be strictly enforced. Not returning books within 30 days after due date will be considered an offense accountable by school regulation.

这段文字是某学校图书馆发布的一篇正式公文，文中使用了四个被动句强调结果，不强调施动者。

（7）避免过多使用名词化词语。

虽然名词比动词和形容词更正式，但是名词化的动词和形容词通常较长，不易理解，应避免过多使用。

例如：The impotence of medical services to change life expectancy and insignificance of much contemporary clinical care in the curing of disease are all obvious, well-documented.（名词化）

- It is all obvious and well-documented that medical services are unable to change life expectancy and much contemporary clinical care is not significant in the curing of disease.（非名词化）

18.4 多样性（Variety）

多样性是指在写作中使用各种不同的句型和不同的结构，避免文章呆板和单调。

18.4.1 句子结构类型（Structural Type）

1. 简单句（Simple sentence）

简单句，即只有一个主谓结构的句子。除了特殊情况，英语句子都有主语、谓语（或表语），有时还有宾语，一般情况下主谓宾的顺序是固定的。但是简单句并不意味着一句中的主语和谓语只有一个，并列主语或并列谓语同样属于简单句。

例如：

- Mom and I went shopping and came home.
- Both Tim and Jane enjoy rock music.
- We sang and danced throughout the night.
- My dad is an engineer.
- We have lived in the city for over 10 years.
- It is important to learn a foreign language.

2. 并列句（Compound sentences）

并列句就是两个或以上的简单句，由表示并列关系的连词或标点连接而成。常见的连词有：and、but、yet、or、nor、for、so、not only … but also、neither … nor …、either … or …、otherwise、while 等。

例如：

- My father is an engineer, and my mother is a teacher.
- I like tea, but he likes coffee.
- I'm thirsty, for it is hot.
- She has a test tomorrow morning, so she cannot go to the party tonight.
- We must hurry, or we will miss the flight.
- The book is quite expensive; it is not worth it.

3. 复杂句（Complex sentences）

复杂句通常由两个以上句子构成，但与并列句不同的是，句子之间有主句和从句关系，一般由关系引导词引导。各分句之间的意义紧密相连，不能简单地把句子拆开理解，而应将各部分综合理解。英文中的从句主要包括主语从句、宾语从句、表语从句、同位语从句、定语从句（限定性和非限定性），以及状语从句（表时间、地点、原因、条件、目的、让步、方式、结果等）。

例如：

- How this accident happened is still unclear.（主语从句）
- I wonder what he is doing over there.（宾语从句）

- The problem is that I have lost his phone number.（表语从句）
- They were very much worried over the fact that you were sick.（同位语从句）
- Mrs. May, who was my former math teacher, retired last year.（非限定性定语从句）
- We arrived the day that they left.（限定性定语从句）
- When the teacher entered the classroom, the students were all talking and laughing.（时间状语从句）
- You can sit wherever you like.（地点状语从句）
- He was quite disappointed because he didn't get the job.（原因状语从句）
- You may borrow my book as long as you keep it clean.（条件状语从句）
- She left early, so that she could make it on time.（目的状语从句）
- Although she felt ill, she still went to work.（让步状语从句）
- You must do it exactly the same as I have shown you.（方式状语从句）
- He was so worried that he couldn't sleep.（结果状语从句）

4. 混合句（Complex/Compound sentences）

混合句，即并列句+复杂句，通常由两个以上简单句及一个以上从句构成。

例如：

- After the earthquake, many people had to relocate, but he chose to stay.
- When my father came home, I was doing my homework, and my mom was cooking in the kitchen.

18.4.2 句子修辞类型（Rhetorical Type）

1. 松散句（Loose sentence）

松散句一般先讲重要信息，后讲次要信息。这种句子在写作上可以起到开门见山的作用，是常见的句子结构，特别适用于文章开头或段落开头，用来提出观点或意见等。

例如：

- The course was not very difficult, although I didn't receive a high grade.
- She later got married and had two children, according to newspaper reports.

2. 圆周句（Periodic sentence）

圆周句，也叫掉尾句，是指作者把最重要的信息放到句末来表达的句子结构。圆周句在结构上是先讲次要信息，后讲重要信息，起到制造悬念的作用。如果读者不看完整的句子，就无法了解句子的重要信息。圆周句在写作中不能通篇使用，一般只是在作者需要强调某个重要信息或引起读者注意时使用。但是在写作中，我们有时可以刻意使用圆周句来丰富文章的句子结构。请对比表 18-1 中的句子：

表 18-1 松散句与圆周句

松散句	圆周句
We need to go shopping today.	Today, we need to go shopping.
She answered all the questions correctly in the pop quiz.	In the pop quiz, she answered all the questions correctly.
She filled the bucket with water to put out the fire.	To put out the fire, she filled the bucket with water.
You will eventually succeed if you put your heart in it.	If you put your heart in it, you will eventually succeed.

3. 平衡句（Balanced sentences）

平衡句是指句中词组或从句有相似结构、意义或长度，前后平衡。由于句子前后对称，经常可用于凸显呼应或对比关系。平衡句可以用来丰富句子结构，但是同样不宜过多使用。

例如：

- Most people marry for love; some marry for money.
- She works as a doctor during the week and a volunteer during the weekend.

18.4.3 句子多样化技巧（Skills in Sentence Variety）

英语句子多样化的方法很多，通过不断变化句子的开头，交替使用长句和短句，变换使用松散句和圆周句，我们可以使文章句子更丰富、内容更生动。但是句子结构不宜生搬硬套，使用什么样的句式结构，主要取决于句子要表达的含义。

1. 并列句还是复杂句

并列句与复杂句可以表达相似含义，但又不完全相同。两者的区别在于强调的重点不同。并列句连词前后重心平衡，没有强调某个重点；而复杂句有主从关系，主句一般为强调部分。

例如：My big brother is in college, and my little sister is still in kindergarten.（并列句）

While my big brother is in college, my little sister is still in kindergarten.（复杂句）

可以看出，例句中的并列句前后两句重要性相同，只是陈述了两个人的现状。而复杂句陈述的重点是妹妹的现状，哥哥的现状只是从属部分，用于状态对比。

2. 松散句、圆周句还是平衡句

松散句是英文写作中主要使用的句子，表义清晰，直截了当。但是通篇过多的松散句会让文章内容松散，读起来乏味。圆周句和平衡句偶尔使用，主要用于强调、对比或变化句式。圆周句和平行句同样不宜过多使用。圆周句比松散句更有重点，但是如果每句都强调，相当于没有强调。另外，圆周句重点靠后，前面是对后面的铺垫，因此读者阅读会比较吃力。平行句同样可以用来达到一定效果，但是过多使用同样会让文章单调无聊。因此，以松散句为主，以圆周句和平衡句为辅，穿插使用，是写作的主要策略。

3. 句子多样化方法

- 如果无需强调，可用 and、but、or、nor、yet、for、so 等连词合并简单句；
- 合并简单句主语，把次要信息变为从句，如使用关系代词 which、who、whoever、whom、that、whose 等，或使用以 after、although、as、as if、because、before、even if、even though、if、if only、rather than、since、that、though、unless、until、when、where、whereas、wherever、whether、which、while 等从属连词引导的状语从句。
- 用介词短语或分词短语表达次要信息。有系动词（am、is、are、was、were 等）的简单句可改为分词短语（由现在分词或过去分词引导），如 speaking of something、knowing something、surprised by something 等。
- 句首使用从属分句或短语，避免每句话使用相同的主语或结构。
- 交替使用长短句。

例如：Tom couldn't sleep. He was worried about the exam next morning.

可改为：

- Tom couldn't sleep, for he was worried about the exam next morning.（使用连词 for）
- Worrying about the exam next morning, Tom couldn't sleep.（使用现在分词）
- Unfortunately, Tom couldn't sleep because he was worried about the exam next morning.（使用副词开头）
- Since Tom was worried about the exam next morning, he couldn't sleep.（使用从属连词）
- The reason why Tom couldn't sleep is that he was worried about the exam next morning.（使用从句）

再如：

I got up a little late on Sunday morning. I washed and had a quick breakfast. Then I started going to town to buy a dictionary. It was recommended by my teacher. All the buses were crowded. I had to wait for a long time. We got off the bus at a busy street an hour later. There were three bookstores there. I went to the first one and didn't find the dictionary. I went to the second one and the dictionary was sold out. I finally bought the dictionary at the third bookstore.

本段中出现了大量简单句，主语和谓语重复频繁，语言啰唆、单调乏味。可以改为：

I got up a little late on Sunday morning. After washing and a quick breakfast, I started going to town to buy the dictionary recommended by the teacher. All the buses were crowded, and I had to wait for a long time. An hour later, I got off at a busy street where there were three bookstores. I went to the first one and didn't find the dictionary. In the second one I was told that the dictionary had been sold out. It was in the third that I finally bought the dictionary.

写作实践 Writing Tasks

▶▶ Revise the sentences to add unity and coherence to the sentences.

(1) The project was costly, and it was a complete success.

(2) The report is chiefly about inflationary trends in the last decade and that the consumer has lost confidence in the quality of many products.

(3) Driving to Chicago that night, a sudden thought struck me.

(4) While many people adore computer games, some others condemn it as an utter waste of time.

(5) Because each year our children spend increasingly more time on computer and TV screens, you need to limit their viewing hours and encourage them to go outdoors and play.

(6) The car accident injured two people, and one person was killed.

▶▶ Revise the following sentences to make them more concise.

(1) Have you ever made a speech in front of a group of people? If you haven't made a speech in front of a group of people, imagine what it is like to make a speech in front of one thousand people.

(2) She enjoyed writing poems, but she wrote poems in secret. She passed away when she was 56 years old. Before she passed away, no one knew she had written over 1,000 poems.

▶▶ Revise the following passage to add variety.

My father is an electrical engineer. My mother was a math teacher. Now she has retired. My sister loves science. She likes solving problems. She was probably influenced by our parents. I like language. I like dealing with people. I don't like working with machines. I don't know why. Now I'm a language teacher. At least I'm a teacher like my mother. I guess that's her influence on me.

第 19 单元 语法
Unit 19 Grammar

学习目标 Learning Objectives

1. 了解常见的语法错误；
2. 学习修改并避免六种常见的语法错误。

课前任务 Pretask

仔细观察下面的句子，检查这些句子的语法是否正确，并做修改。

- To find a place where I can park my car.
- I went to the grocery, I bought some food.
- At the age often, my grandfather passed away.
- Speaking on the phone, the car ran into a tree.
- Neither the driver nor the passengers was to be blamed.
- When you write the beginning, we should make it appealing.

引言 Introduction

　　写作最基本的要求就是语法与拼写准确。如果一篇作文中反复出现多处语法错误，那么无论你的观点多么吸引人，立意多么新颖，内容多么精彩，这都只是一篇有缺陷的文章，读者对文章的整体印象会大打折扣，甚至反感。因此可以说，没有好的语法，就没有好的写作。

　　语法是英语学习中的重点，内容繁多。本单元介绍英语写作中最常出现的六种语法错误：残缺句（fragments）、粘连句（run-ons）、错置修饰语（misplaced modifiers）、悬垂修饰语（dangling modifiers）、主谓一致错误（sentence agreement mistakes），以及时态、人称及句式一致问题。这些是出现频率最高的语法错误，会影响句子结构甚至句义。

知识要点 Key Knowledge

19.1 残缺句（Fragment）

残缺句，也叫破句、片段句、碎片句，是指一个不完整的句子。残缺句有很多形式，常见的残缺句主要有四种：从属连词残缺句（dependent-word fragments）、现在分词残缺句（-ing fragments）、增加细节残缺句（added-detail fragments）及缺少主语残缺句（missing-subject fragments）。从结构上说，一个完整的英文句子应当包括至少一个主语和一个谓语，主语是施动的人或物，谓语是动作本身。而残缺句则是一个缺少主语或谓语动词，或是缺少完整意义的词群。

例如：

*Mr. Smith gone to the hospital.（缺谓语）

*To find a parking space there usually easy during the week.（缺谓语）

*Living in the middle of nowhere.（缺谓语）

*Many young people who leave home at an early age.（缺谓语）

*His work been so busy that he has little time for his family.（缺谓语）

19.1.1 从属连词残缺句（Dependent-Word Fragment）

从属连词残缺句是由 after、because、even though、which 等从属连词引导的句子独立出现而导致的。这些句子需要另一个句子来补充，使句义完整。

例如：

*Because I have a test tomorrow morning.

*Even though I have a test tomorrow morning.

*After I have the test tomorrow morning.

*Which is because I have a test tomorrow morning.

这些句子句义都不完整，只可作为一个完整句子的一部分。这类残缺句的修改方法一般有两种，在句子之前或之后补充一个句子，或去掉从属连词。

例如：

- I cannot go to the party tonight, because I have a test tomorrow morning.
- I went to the party today, even though I have a test tomorrow morning.
- After I have the test tomorrow, I'm going to hold a party.

- I have my reason, which is because I have a test tomorrow morning.
- I cannot go to the party. It is because I have a test tomorrow morning.
- I have a test tomorrow morning.

19.1.2 现在分词残缺句（-ing Fragment）

现在分词残缺句是现在分词引导的词群单独成句所造成的残缺句，这类残缺句经常缺少主语和部分谓语。

例如：*Trying to find her cat.（缺主语和部分谓语）

　　　*My brother running a restaurant for five years.（缺部分谓语）

此类残缺句一般有两种修改方法，在句子之前或之后补充一个句子，补充主语并将 -ing 动词修改为正确形式。

例如：

- The woman looked around the campus, trying to find her cat.
- The woman tried to find her cat.
- My brother has been running a restaurant for five years.
- Running a restaurant for five years, my brother has saved enough money for a new apartment.

19.1.3 增加细节残缺句（Added-detail Fragment）

增加细节残缺句是由 also、especially、except、for example、like、including、such as 等词引导的句子独立出现而导致的残缺句，通常缺少主语及动词。

例如：*Especially if there are children listening.

*For lunch, I often eat fast food. Such as hamburger or fried chicken.

*You'll need a variety of skills. Including leadership and negotiating.

此类残缺句的修改方法：在残缺句之前补充一个句子，并用逗号连接；用逗号使残缺句与前面句子相连，或添加主语及动词。

例如：

- You have to be careful about what you say, especially if there are children listening.
- For lunch, I often eat fast food, such as hamburger or fried chicken.
- You'll need a variety of skills, including leadership and negotiating.

19.1.4 缺少主语残缺句（Missing-Subject Fragment）

主语残缺句是缺少主语的词群独立成句造成的残缺句。

例如：*Lily loves drawing. But hates singing.

此类残缺句的修改方法：用逗号使残缺句与前面句子相连，或添加主语。

例如：

- Lily loves drawing, but hates singing.
- Lily loves drawing. But she hates singing.

19.2 粘连句（Run-on Sentence）

粘连句是指数个独立的分句（有完整主谓的句子）在没有标点或错误标点的情况下，黏连在一起。粘连句分两种：无标点粘连句（fused sentences）、逗号粘连句（comma splices）。

无标点粘连句是指两个独立句中没有标点分割，如：

*The bus arrived I got onto it.

*I had a fever my mom was worried.

逗号粘连句是指用逗号连接两个独立的句子，这种是最常见的。受中文影响，学生经常会使用逗号连接一串独立的句子，如：

*The bus arrived, I got onto it.

*I had a fever, my mom was worried.

粘连句的四种修改方法：

（1）用句号及大写字母分割句子，如：

- The bus arrived. I got onto it.
- I had a fever. My mom was worried.

（2）使用逗号及连词（and、but、for、or、nor、so、yet），如：

- The bus arrived, and I got onto it.
- I had a fever, so my mom was worried.

（3）使用分号连接两个独立句子，如：

- The bus arrived; I got onto it.
- I had a fever; my mom was worried.

（4）使用从属结构，让一个句子从属于另一个句子，如：

- As soon as the bus arrived, I got onto it.
- Due to the fact that I had a fever, my mom was worried.

19.3 错置修饰语（Misplaced Modifiers）

错置修饰语是指因为修饰语的位置不正确而导致句子错误或句义不清。在英语中，修饰语应紧靠它所修饰的词语，如果放错了位置，就会造成意义上的误解。错置修饰语主要分为状语错置、定语错置及修饰语错置。

（1）状语错置主要是状语位置错误引起的语义混淆，如：

*At the age of five my mother began to teach me English.

"at the age of five"置于句首会让读者误认为在"my mother"只有 5 岁，可改为：My mother began to teach me English when I was five.

（2）定语错置主要是定语位置错误引起的语义混淆，如：

*A horse was almost hit by a car which jumped over the fence.

"which jumped over the fence"本来是修饰 horse 的，而在句中用来修饰 car，是误置，可改为：A horse which jumped over the fence was almost hit by a car.

（3）修饰语错置主要是修饰语位置错误引起的语义混淆，如：

*Tim was spotted by his teacher cheating in the exam.

此句中的"cheating in the exam"应修饰 Tim，而不是 teacher，可改为：Tim was spotted cheating in the exam by his teacher.

注意：误置修饰语与歧义修饰语（squinting modifier）略有不同，后者是指因在句中位置不当而导致语义歧义的修饰语，如：

*The girl who had been dancing gracefully entered the room.

这句中的修饰语 gracefully 是修饰 dancing 还是 entered 呢？这两种情况都有可能，为明确起见，可根据句义改为：

- The girl who had been gracefully dancing entered the room.（修饰 dancing）
- The girl who had been dancing entered the room gracefully.（修饰 entered）

19.4 悬垂修饰语（Dangling Modifiers）

悬垂修饰语是指句首的短语与后文句子的逻辑关系混乱不清，尤其指句首短语的逻辑

主语与其后句子的主语不一致，如：

*While eating breakfast, my cat sat on my laps.

读者可能将本句理解为我的猫吃早餐时坐在我的腿上。但句子本意是，我吃早餐时，我的猫坐在我的腿上。

悬垂结构主要有两种修改方法：将后半句主语更换为本意所指的主语，或在前半句加主语，如：

- While eating breakfast, I sat with my cat on my laps.
- While I was eating breakfast, my cat sat on my laps.

19.5 主谓一致错误（Sentence Agreement Mistake）

主谓一致即谓语动词在人称和数上要和主语保持一致。主谓一致错误主要发生在谓语动词单复数的使用上。判断主谓是否一致，首先应找到句子主语。主谓一致一般包括三类：语法一致、意义一致和就近一致。

（1）语法一致即谓语动词在单复数形式上要和主语保持一致，如：

- Both products have their own advantages.
- The man has two kids.

（2）意义一致指谓语动词要和主语意义上的单复数保持一致，如：

- The family are all fond of basketball.
- The family is the smallest cell of the society.

（3）就近一致就是谓语动词要和靠近它的主语部分保持一致，如：

- Not only he but also all his family are keen on music.
- Neither his family nor he knows anything about the news.

下面介绍主谓一致的一些常见问题。

19.5.1 以 s 结尾的名词作主语时的主谓一致（Sentence Agreement When Subjects Are Nouns Ending With "s"）

（1）以 s 结尾的疾病名称（如 arthritis、bronchitis、diabetes、mumps、phlebitis、rickets）和游戏名称通常当单数用，如：

- Arthritis is a disease causing pain in the joints of the body.
- Darts is a popular game.

但当 Darts、Marbles 等这种意义为游戏器具而非游戏名称时，谓语动词通常用作复数，如：

- Three darts are thrown at each turn.
- Ten marbles are needed for this game.

（2）以 s 结尾的地理名称、国名等用单数，如：

- The United States is a Pacific country.
- The Netherlands was hit by a storm.

但如果是群岛、山脉、海峡、瀑布等地理名称作主语，谓语动词用作复数，如：

- The West Indies are commonly divided into two parts.
- The Niagara Falls are made up of several smaller falls.
- The Himalayas are the highest mountains in the world.

（3）以 ics 结尾的学科名称（如 physics、mathematics、mechanics、optics、acoustics、politics、statistics、economics、linguistics、athletics 等），通常作单数用，如：

- Physics is an important discipline.
- Mathematics is the basis of many other subjects.
- Linguistics is a course studied by all English-major students.

（4）其他以 s 结尾的名词：

① 由两个部分组成的物体名称通常是以 s 结尾，如 scissors、trousers、glasses、pincers、pliers、shorts、suspenders 等，这类名词通常作复数用；带"一把、一条"等的则作单数用。

- The scissors need to be sharpened.
- My new shoes are all dirty.
- One pair of scissors isn't enough.
- How much is this pair of shoes?

② 以 s 结尾的 contents、fireworks、goods、stairs 等名词，通常作复数，如：

- The contents of today's course are a bit hard to understand.
- The goods are in good condition.

③ 由 ings 结尾的名词，如 earrings、diggings、surroundings 等，通常用作复数，如：

- Her earrings are quite unique.
- The surroundings are mainly trees.

④ 以 s 结尾的单复数同形的名词，如 species、remains 等，随后动词的单复数形式取决于这些名词是用作单数还是复数，如：

- A new species of butterfly has been found in Africa.
- There are over 1,000 species of fish.

⑤ 以 s 结尾的不可数名词，如 news，通常用作单数，如：

- The news of the tragedy is spreading fast.

19.5.2　集合名词作主语时的主谓一致（Sentence Agreement When Subject Are Collective Nouns）

（1）作复数的集合名词，如 police、cattle、people、faculty、flock 等，通常用复数，如：

- The police are here.
- People are gathering.

（2）作不可数名词的集合名词，如 machinery、equipment、merchandise 等，通常用单数，如：

- The machinery is driven by electricity.
- This equipment has turned out to be useful.

（3）既可作单数也可作复数的集合名词，如 class、family、public、team、crew、board、herd、committee、party、jury、enemy、audience 等。根据语境，若把这个集合名词所代表的人或事物看作一个整体，就是单数，用单数动词；若把它所代表的人或事物看作若干个个体的话，就是复数，用复数动词，如：

- The family is a happy one.
- My family all like watching basketball.

（4）"a committee of/the board of 等 + 复数名词"这种结构通常用作单数，如：

- A committee of eight professors is present.
- The board of directors is responsible for the management of the firm.

19.5.3　并列结构作主语时的主谓一致（Sentence Agreement When Subjects Are Parallel Structures）

（1）由 and/both... and 连接的并列主语，通常用作复数，如：

- My dad and I are going to meet my mom at the airport.
- Both John and Linda are working on the issue.

注意：如果作主语的并列结果表示单数意义，则动词用单数，如：

- Ham and egg is a good breakfast.
- A needle and thread was found on the floor.

（2）由 or/either... or/neither nor 等连接的并列主语，随后的动词形式按就近原则处理，如：

- Either the pedestrians or the driver is to be blamed.
- Neither the driver nor the pedestrians are to be blamed.

（3）主语 + as much as/rather than/more than 等引导从句时，随后的动词形式依主语本身的单复数而定，如：

- Some of the workers as much as the manager were responsible for the loss.
- His brother rather than his parents is to blame.
- My wife, more than anyone else in the family, is anxious to go there again.

（4）主语 + as well as/with/together with/except 等引导的词组时，随后的动词形式也取决于主语本身的单复数形式，如：

- His father, as well as his two children, is going to the train station.
- The warehouse, with all its stockings, was burned last night.

- Tom, together with his two brothers, was on that airplane.
- No one except two students was late for the class.

19.5.4 表示数量概念的名词词组作主语的主谓一致（Sentence Agreement When Subjects Are Nouns Showing Quantity）

（1）表示确定数量的名词词组作主语

① 表示时间、金钱、距离、体积、重量、面积、数字等词作主语时，其意义若是指总量，应作单数，谓语动词用单数；如果其意义是指"有多少数量"则应作复数，谓语动词用复数，如：

- Three years is a long time for a little kid.
- Four weeks are often approximately regarded as one month.

② 主语由分数/百分数 + of + 词组构成，其动词的形式依 of 后名词类别而定，如：

- Two thirds of the money was donated.
- Two thirds of the employees are currently working from home.
- Over sixty percent of the city was destroyed in the war.

③ 主语由"one in/one out of+ 复数名词"构成，其后动词通常用单数，如：

- One in(out of) ten students has suffered from some form of depression.

④ 加减乘除运算一般用单数，但加和乘也可用复数，如：

- 30 minus 15 is 15.
- 30 divided by 5 is 6.
- 8 plus 2 is/are 10.
- 9 times 9 is/are 81.

（2）表示非确定数量的名词词组作主语

① 主语由 most of…、some of…、all of… 等构成，其后的动词形式依 of 后名词类别而定，如：

- Most of the money was spent on maintenance.
- Most of the language teachers are women.

- All of his files were destroyed in the fire.

② 主语由 lots of、loads of、plenty of 等构成，其后的动词形式依 of 后名词类别而定，如：

- Lots of food is going to be wasted.
- Lots of children are playing there.

③ 主语由 a portion of、a series of、a pile of 等构成，其后的动词通常用单数形式，如：

- Only a portion of the estate was left to his children.
- A series of mysterious events has happened in this castle.
- A pile of books is waiting for me.

④ 主语由 "many a/more than one + 名词" 等构成，其意义虽属于复数，但随后的动词仍遵循 "语法一致" 原则，用单数，如：

- Many a doctor is busy with their work.
- More than one person is missing.

⑤ 主语由 "an average of/a majority of+ 名词复数" 构成，其后的动词形式通常用复数，如：

- An average of 10 weeks are needed for recovery.
- Polls show that a majority of younger voters support marriage equality.

19.5.5　其他方面的主谓一致（Other Sentence Agreement Issues）

（1）由 what、who、why、that、which 等引导的主语从句中，其后谓语用单数，如：

- What caused the plane crash is still unknown.
- Who is responsible for the incident is to be determined.
- Where to put away all these books is a problem.

① 两个由 and 连接的并列名词性从句作主语表示两件事情，谓语用复数，如：

- What caused the plane crash and who is responsible for it remain a mystery.

② What 引导的主语从句，如果 what 明确指多个东西，则谓语用复数，如：

- What I bought on this trip are some maps and two T-shirts.

（2）用不定代词（someone、somebody、each、either one、everyone、anyone 等）作主语，谓语通常用单数，如：

- Anyone who wants to leave has to ask permission.

（3）由不定式和动名词作主语时，其后的谓语通常用单数，如：

- To live a healthy life is what he's pursuing.
- Jogging is good for cardio functions.

19.6　时态、人称和句式一致错误（Tense, Person and Sentence Structure Agreement Mistakes）

写作中应保持每个句子及前后文时态及人称一致，在平行句中，应保持句式一致，否则可能造成时态、人称和句式上的错误，导致句子混乱。

19.6.1　时态一致（Agreement in Tense）

时态不一致是写作中非常容易犯的一个错误。在英语写作中，应首先确定一个基本时态，是过去、现在还是将来，必要时在进行时态的改变。

例如：*I got up in the morning late. I run out of my room and get in the classroom on time.

本句中时态均应为过去式，应改为：

I got up in the morning late. I ran out of my room and got in the classroom on time.

但当文章内容明显强调时态变化时，可改变时态，如：

- I lived with my parents before; now I live in a dormitory with three other students; in the future, I will have my own family.
- You were, are and will always be the one I love most.

19.6.2　人称一致（Agreement in Person）

例如：*When you read this article, we can find many grammatical and spelling mistakes, and they can make us feel confused.

句中出现了"you、we、us"，前后人称不一致，可改为：

- When we read this article, we can find many grammatical and spelling mistakes, and they can make us feel confused.
- When you read this article, you can find many grammatical and spelling mistakes, and they can make you feel confused.

19.6.3 句式一致（Agreement in Sentence Structure）

在平行结构中，前后句式应保持统一，如：

*I like reading, to jog, and photography.

本句中"like"后是动词 ing 形式，后面跟着 to do 结构，然后又是名词形式，但本句应该是平行结构，故应改为：I like reading, jogging and taking photographs.

写作实践 Writing Tasks

▶▶ Rewrite the following sentences to make them error-free.

(1) Because some students work part-time while taking a full load of courses .

(2) Many young people who leave home at an early age .

(3) The man in the grey woolen jacket.

(4) Walking to school on a cold, windy day.

(5) Although John didn't enjoy going to school.

(6) My mom made some sandwiches and prepares some fruits for the picnic.

(7) I have done all my homework and was able to go to the party tomorrow.

(8) Good interpreters should always be well-prepared and constantly increase his language skills.

(9) The coach told the players to get a lot of sleep, not eating too much, and doing some warm-up exercises before the game.

(10) Now that you are a professional writer, they should be aware of writing sources, consulting usage dictionaries, and to strive to improve their writing style.

▶▶ Rewrite the following sentences to make them error-free both in grammar and in meaning.

(1) He almost worked all day.

(2) The place was discovered where the ship sunk in 1929.

(3) Every six hours the doctor told me to take a pill.

(4) A beautiful scarf was around her shoulder which she bought in Hangzhou.

(5) Fortunately, the fire was put out before any damage was done by the firemen.

Take a quiz

第 20 单元　标点
Unit 20　Punctuation

学习目标 Learning Objectives

1. 了解常见的英文标点符号；
2. 正确使用英文标点符号；
3. 中文与英文标点符号的区别。

课前任务 Pretask

仔细观察下面的句子，判断这些句子的标点使用是否合理，并做出修改。

- In the supermarket, we bought some fruits; vegetables; milk; bread; and soft drink.
- After he left. She started to cry.
- My favorite novel is "Jane Eyre".
- The article is called Three easy ways to lose weight.
- My father said: "You need to be honest."
- He opened the door and left ……

引言 Introduction

掌握正确的标点符号使用方法，既能提高写作技巧，又能彰显写作水平。标点符号虽小，但作用不小，标点错误会影响阅读理解。英语学习者应该掌握正确的英文标点用法，包括逗号、句号、冒号、分号、破折号、连接号、引号、撇号、括号、问号、感叹号、省略号、斜线号等。

知识要点 Key Knowledge

20.1 逗号和句号（Comma & Period）

逗号和句号是写作中出现频率最高的标点符号，中英文中的逗号和句号在使用上略有不同。中文经常用逗号连接一连串的短句，并在一个意群结束时使用句号；而英文在一个完整的句子（即有完整的主谓结构）后就应使用句号，如果直接使用逗号，则会变成上一单元讲到的粘连句。

20.1.1 逗号（，Comma）

英文逗号和中文逗号一样，表示短暂的停顿，主要在以下七种情况中使用：

（1）用在两个由连词 and、but、or、for、so、nor 或 yet 等连接完整的句子之间，如：

- My daughter is four years old, but my son is only one.
- I cannot go to work tomorrow, for I caught a bad cold.

（2）用在状语（从句或短语）和句子主语之间，如：

- Just in time, Mary stopped the car.
- After graduating from college, he joined the army.

（3）用在一系列并列单词或短语之间，如：

- For the barbecue party, we bought pork, chicken breast, shrimp, and some different vegetables.
- She opened the closet, took a jacket, and ran out.
- The room is bright, roomy and comfortable.

注意：

① 连词一般放在最后一个并列结构前，如果并列结构较复杂，应在连词前面加逗号分隔；如果并列结构较简单，都是单词，则连词前面可以不加逗号。

② 很多学生受中文影响会用顿号（、）连接并列结构，但顿号是中文标点，英文中不能出现。

③ 有时并列两个同级别形容词时，可以用逗号替代"and"，如：

- We can see thick, black cloud in the sky.

（4）用在句中插入语处，常见的有同位语、非限定性定语从句、补充信息等，如：

- Dr. White, the chairman of the department, invited us over for dinner.
- Judy's purple necklace, which her husband brought back from Europe, was broken.
- Tom, tired of the cold weather in Minnesota, moved to Florida.
- John, 55, is studying in college.

（5）用于引导直接引语，如：

- The waitress said, "You'll have to wait for 30 minutes."
- "No comment," said the man.

注意：

① 当引文在后时，即便前面是逗号，引文中首字母须大写。
② 如果引文在前，讲话人在后，则引文以逗号结尾。
③ 直接引文末尾的标点应放在引号内。
④ 学生受中文影响常会用冒号+引号表示引文，而英文则应使用逗号+引号。

（6）用在连接性副词 however、meanwhile、in fact、in addition、moreover、nevertheless、as a result、thus、therefore、for example、finally、in other words 等后面，如果这些词出现在句中，一般前后都需逗号，如：

- However, Mary doesn't like speaking in public.
- Mary, however, doesn't like speaking in public.

（7）用在一些习惯用法中，如 Yes 或 No 后、反问句前、年份前、数字中、人名后、城市和省份（州）之间、国家之间、信件中的人名等，如：

- Yes, I think so.
- She's angry, isn't she?
- November 23, 2018
- 675,010,012
- Paul, I think you are right.
- Xi'an, Shaanxi Province
- Beijing, China
- Sincerely yours,

- Dear Robert,
- Washington, George

注意：英文人名一般名在前、姓在后，中间没有逗号。但有时在名单、参考文献中，为了排序或突出姓氏，也可把姓放前、名放后，中间用逗号分隔。

20.1.2 句号（. Period）

和中文一样，句号最重要的功能是结束一个句子。中文句号是空心点（。），英文句号是实心点（.），不可混用。英文句号主要有以下两种用法：

（1）用于有完整主谓的句子、语气较弱的祈使句、间接疑问句后，如：

- Every complete sentence should have a subject and a predicate.
- Write in a complete sentence.
- They asked how the food was.

（2）用于缩略词后，如：

- Mrs. and Mr.
- U.S.A.

20.2 冒号和分号（Colon & Semi-colon）

20.2.1 冒号（: Colon）

冒号的功能和中文相似，主要作用是引起读者注意。冒号主要有三种用法：

（1）用于引导一个序列，如：

- Three people were awarded: John Smith, Tom Andrews and Mary Anderson.

（2）用于强调后面的词或句子，如：

- She had only one thing on her mind: going home.
- The news was devastating: No one had survived the plane crash.

注意：冒号后如果是完整的句子，首字母一般需大写。

（3）用于引导含有多个句子的较长引文，如：

President Xi Jinping said: "The world needs a stable Central Asia. The sovereignty, security, independence and territorial integrity of Central Asian countries must be upheld; their people's choice of development paths must be respected; and their efforts for peace, harmony and tranquility must be supported."

20.2.2 分号（；Semi-colon）

分号（；）和冒号（：）虽长相相似，但作用完全不同。分号和逗号一样，用于句子的停顿，但是分隔程度介于逗号和句号之间。分号主要有以下三种用法：

（1）用于连接两个完整的句子，中间没有连词。在这种情况下，分号可与句号互换，但是分号更强调两个句子之间的紧密联系，如：

- Tom borrowed my car; he broke it.
- Tom borrowed my car. He broke it.

（2）用于连接性副词 however、therefore、hence、nevertheless、moreover、thus、otherwise、besides 等之前。连接性副词不可做复合句中的连词使用，前面应当使用分号或句号，如：

- The ride was quite bumpy; therefore, Maggie didn't enjoy it at all.
- The ride was quite bumpy. However, the kids seemed to be enjoying it.

（3）用于本身含有逗号的并列结构，如：

- I made quite a handsome amount of money this summer: by walking dogs, I made $200; by babysitting, I made $300; and by selling biscuits, I made $100.

20.3 破折号和连接号（Dash & Hyphen）

破折号（—或 –）和连接号（-）虽长相相似，但是作用完全不同，应避免混淆。

20.3.1 破折号（—或 – Dash）

英文破折号的作用和中文类似，通常做强调、解释或者补充说明。英文破折号分为两种：长破折号 Em dash(—) 和短破折号 En dash (–)。En dash 的长度是 Em dash 的一半。长破折号主要有以下六种用法：

（1）用于强调、解释或补充信息，当用于句中时，前后应各有一个破折号，如：

- The new shopping mall will open Tuesday—if the air-conditioning works.
- His dream—to have a house, a dog and a loved one—was never realized.

（2）用于表示比逗号长的停顿或语气改变，如：

- I sure could not stand his behavior—but who could?

（3）用于表示未完或打断的句子，如：

- Your job is—

（4）用于体现戏剧化效果，如：

- I was so tired I fell asleep—standing up.

（5）用于表示引言，如：

- —What are you doing?
  —I'm writing my essay.

（6）用于引导副标题或在引言后标注作者，如：

- A wise man will make more opportunities than he finds.

—Francis Bacon

短破折号主要用于连接数字表示起止范围（比如 1:00–2:00 pm），以及表示两者之间的关系和联系（如 Boston–Hartford route）。

20.3.2 连接号（-Hyphen）

连接号的长度比短破折号（En dash）还要短，主要用于行末单词换行以及连接复合词的各个组成部分，主要有五种用法：

（1）用于复合词中，或连接字母或单词，表示意义紧密相连，如：

- A-type
- she-male
- pork-chop
- S-H-O-P
- co-worker
- a well-prepared plan
- a 20-mile search area

（2）表示型号，如：

- This model, PNT-QE-0725, is no longer in use.

（3）避免词义混淆，如：

- She recovered the torn seat.
- She re-covered the torn seat.
- He is a small business man.
- He is a small-business man.

（4）连接多个单词，表示含义合并，如：

- Don't be all my-life-sucks-and-everyone-hates-me.
- That I'm-good-at-nothing-attitude isn't going to help you.

（5）用于行末单词换行。注意：换行时应在音节处切分，不可随意切分。切分后第一行字母的末尾加连接号，第二行的开头不加连接号。一般六个字母以下的单词，不建议换行。

20.4 引号和撇号（Quotation Mark & Apostrophe）

20.4.1 引号（" " Quotation Mark）

英文引号同中文，主要表示引言或短作品名，主要有以下用法：

（1）表示直接引语，如：

- Martin Luther King Jr. once said, "I have a dream…"

（2）表示作品名，如书名、报纸名、杂志中的文章名、书中的章节名、短故事名、诗歌名及歌曲名。

- I was deeply impressed by his article *Music and Neurology*.

注意：书名、报纸名、期刊名、杂志名等长作品名应使用斜体（打印）或下划线（手写）。

（3）强调、区别某个单词或表讽刺含义，如：

- What is the difference between "marry" and "merry"?
- The so-called "expert" turned out to be a fake.

（4）当引文中再出现引文或短作品名时，可使用单引号，如：

- The professor said, "For class on Friday, please read the article titled 'culture and language' on page 15."

注意：逗号和句号应放在引号内；破折号、问号、感叹号等如果属于引文，则应放在引号内；如果不属于引文，则放在引号外。冒号和分号应放在引号外。

20.4.2　撇号（'Apostrophe）

（1）表示所属关系，如：

- Mary's dad was in hospital.
- The fireman's arm was injured.

（2）表示缩略字母或年份，如：

- I'll never forget you.
- He won't come.
- finger lickin' good
- The class of '97
- the '90s

20.5　括号（Parenthesis & Brackets）

英文中的括号包括圆括号和方括号，括号永远应成对出现，不能只有单边括号。

20.5.1　圆括号（( ) Parenthesis）

圆括号用法同中文，主要用于包含相关但相对不重要的补充信息，可以是词语、短语或句子，如：

- The government's education report (April 2005) shows that the level of literacy is rising in nearly all areas.
- I visited Kathmandu (which was full of tourists) on my way to the Himalayas.
- You can eat almost anything while travelling if you are careful to observe simple rules (Avoiding unboiled water is one of the main rules to be aware of).

括号内的内容可能影响理解，不宜使用过多。如果括号内为单词或短语，句号应放在括号外；如果括号内容为句子，且句子内容是主句的一部分，则不需要标点，首字母不大写；如果括号内容为句子，且独立于主句，则应将句号放在括号内，首字母大写，如：

- Place a period outside a closing parenthesis if the material inside is not a sentence (such as a phrase).
- If a parenthetical sentence (as can be seen in this example) is part of a sentence, don't capitalize the first word.
- If the material in the parentheses is an independent sentence, place the period before the closing parenthesis. (Here is an example.)

20.5.2 方括号（[ ] Brackets）

方括号主要用来表示引言中暗含的内容，即因有上下文，所以在引言中没有说出，但是如果不作注释，读者可能不易理解，如：

John said, "We went [to the international import expo], and had a good time."
"We support the [Greenville County] council's decision," she said.

20.6 其它 (Others)

20.6.1 问号和感叹号（？&！Question Mark & Exclamation Mark）

英文问号（Question mark）和感叹号（Exclamation mark）用法同中文。注意：直接问句用问号，而间接问句不用问号。如果是多个问句，可以在最后一句使用问号。如需强调每个问句，也可以在每个句子后使用问号，如：

- Did you review the course, do your homework and preview the next chapter?
- Did you review the course? Do your homework? Preview the next chapter?

20.6.2 省略号（... Ellipsis）

英文省略号用法同中文，表示未完或断续的句子。但是英文中的省略号是三个英文点号，中文是六个点号，如：

- I'm forgetting… my homework!
- Hey… good to see you.
- I wonder what I can say to him after…
- Do you like me…?

20.6.3 斜线号（／Slash or Virgule）

（1）表示"or"，如：

- cat/dog
- and/or
- s/he
- his/her

（2）表示固定搭配，如：

- 80 miles/hour
- student/teacher ratio
- w/o

（3）表示共同属性，如：

- Spartanburg/Greenville airport（表示两个地区的共用机场）
- The March/April issue of the journal（表示三四月合刊）
- The innovative classroom/laboratory（表示既是教室，又是实验室）

写作实践 Writing Tasks

▶▶ **Fill in the blanks.**

(1) A _____ often marks a slight pause in a sentence.

(2) A _____ marks the end of a sentence.

(3) _____ are used to indicate someone's exact words or the title of short works.

(4) We can use a _____ to mark off items in a series when the items themselves contain commas.

(5) To signal a pause longer than a comma, or a change in tone, we can use a _____.

(6) _____ has the same function in handwriting as italics in typing.

(7) Names of articles in journals should be in _____.

(8) In Chinese, we often use commas in between a series of thoughts, and end with a period; while in English, _____ are used to mark the end of each complete sentence.

▶▶ **Put the correct punctuation marks in the spaces underlined in the following paragraphs.**

Harvard University is a private_ Ivy League research university in Cambridge_ Massachusetts_ Established 1636_ its history_ influence and wealth have made it one of the world's most prestigious universities_

The University is organized into eleven separate academic units_ten faculties and the Radcliffe Institute for Advanced Study_with campuses throughout the Boston metropolitan area_ its 209_acre _ 85 ha_ main campus is centered on Harvard Yard in Cambridge_ approximately 3 miles _5 km_ northwest of Boston_ the business school and athletics facilities_ including Harvard Stadium_ are located across the Charles River in the Allston neighborhood of Boston and the medical_ dental_ and public health schools are in the Longwood Medical Area_ Harvard_s $37.6 billion financial endowment is the largest of any academic institution_